PRACTICAL
BALINESE

a communication guide

PRACTICAL BALINESE

a communication guide
by Günter Spitzing

PERIPLUS

ISBN 962-593-068-X

Publisher: Eric. M. Oey
Author and cover illustrator: Günter Spitzing
Editor: Thomas G. Oey
Co-editor: Rev. N. Shadeg SVD, Yayasan Widya Wahana (Widya Wahana Foundation)
Production: Violet Wong

Distributors:
Asia Pacific: Berkeley Books Pte.Ltd., 5 Little Road #08-01, Singapore 536983.
Indonesia: PT Java Books Indonesia, Jl. Gading Kirana I Blok A 14 No.17, Kelapa Gading Kirana, Jakarta 14240
U.S.A.: Tuttle Publishing, Distribution Center, Airport Industrial Park, 364 Innovation Drive, North Clarendon, VT 05759-9436

Second Printing, April 2002
Printed in Indonesia

Acknowledgment:
Many thanks to Made Buwana, Ubud, who gave me a lot of important information about the Balinese language and proofread the Balinese terms in the book.

Contents ✧✧✧✧✧✧✧✧✧✧✧✧✧✧✧

Contents

Foreword ✧ ✧ ✧ ✧ ✧ ✧ ✧ ✧ ✧ ✧ ✧ ✧ ✧ ✧ ✧

Bali is indeed a lovely and colorful island. As a foreigner arriving here, you enthusiastically take in
with mind and heart all the bright shining colors
and picturesque events. You have to use your eyes
and perhaps your camera too. But how can you look
directly into the hearts of the *anak Bali*—people of
Bali? It can be done! You only have to talk with them
in their own *basa Bali*—the Balinese language. If you
can commit to memory 150 Balinese words, you will
open doors of discovery in Bali you would never
have otherwise.

This booklet is not only a language guide, but a
brief cultural introduction to this enchanted island,
which is replete with fine arts and skilful perfor-
mances.

If you are staying only three days in Bali and if you
have just such a little bit of interest in cultural
events you will have learned automatically some
kruna (words)—for example:

pura	Hindu temple
puri	palace, but can refer to a simple house of a member of the *ksatria*, the ruling and warriors caste.
wayang kulit	shadow play (Lit: performance–leather)
topeng	(wooden) mask, mime performance with masks.

There are three languages spoken in Bali:

1. **English** naturally is the lingua franca. Nearly everybody in the main tourist centers speaks some English. You may mix English with the *kruna Bali*. For example, a good phrase to use is *sing kēnkēn* — no problem (Lit: Not what-what!)!

2. **Indonesian, *Bahasa Indonesia*,** is the national language spoken all over the archipelago's nearly +/- 14,000 islands. Everybody on the *nusa dewata Bali* (Lit: island of deities Bali) speaks it—with the exception of the older people. Much of the vocabulary of Indonesian and Balinese is quite different—perhaps as different as English and German, for example. But the grammatical structures are quite similar, because Indonesian and Balinese and most other regional languages in the Southeast Asian and South Pacific islands are members of the same Malayo–Austronesian language family. So, if you already know some Indonesian you might try replacing this or that Indonesian phrase with a Balinese one you have just learned. All Balinese must know the Indonesian language, for Indonesian is the language of modern and public life. If for example they visit a *kantor pos* (Indonesian: post office) to buy a *peranko* (Indonesian: stamp) they use Indonesian, because of the lack of Balinese terms. Balinese is the language of home life, of farming, of culture and of religion.

3. ***Basa Bali*** is the mother language of the people of Bali, of some parts of Western Lombok and some vil-

Foreword ✧ ✧ ✧ ✧ ✧ ✧ ✧ ✧ ✧ ✧ ✧ ✧ ✧ ✧ ✧ ✧

lages inhabited by "transmigrated" Balinese in Sulawesi—altogether approximately three million people. So *i mêmê* (the mother) and *i bapa* (the father) is speaking *tekên pianakne luh* to his or her little girl (Lit: child—female—his) and *anak muani* boy. *I anak Bali* (the men of Bali) express their feelings in their *basa Bali*. Usually the Balinese don't expect a *tamiu* (visitor, guest) to be able to speak some of their language—but nonetheless they will appreciate it very much, if you do.

If you already have some familiarity with the island, you may know more *basa Bali* than you think. There are several *kruna Bali* that we are already very familiar with. For example, borrowed words from Balinese or related languages:

gambelan	gamelan orchestra
gong	gong
padi	rice growing on the field (paddy-field)
nasi	boiled rice
satê	satai, small meat pieces on skewers
batik	batik, cloths dyed by a special handicraft method
keris	keris, the ceremonial Balinese or Javanese dagger/sword.

Or we can understand Indo–European words of Indian (Sanskrit) origin:

nama	name
madia	middle (the middle part of the human body)

The *basa Bali alus* (lit: language-Bali-very distinguished) in particular possesses a lot of words from Sanskrit, which we will easily recognize if we are just a little bit familiar with Indian culture or history:

guru	teacher
pedanda	brahmana priest (Indian: *pandit*)
naga	mythological snake, dragon
meru	pagodalike wooden building with grass/ijuk roofs, 3 until 11 roofs in temple yards (called after the Indian holy Mount Meru)
brahmana	highest caste (Indian: *brahmin*)
ksatria	ruler and warrior, second caste (Indian: *kshatrya*)
wesia	merchants and officials, third caste (Indian: *weysha*)
sudra	rice farmers 'caste' (sudra: non-caste), majority (nearly 95%) of the Hindu population in Bali (Indian: *shudra*). Nevertheless Balinese prefer the native word *jaba* (outsider).

Pronunciation Guide ⇦⇦⇦ ⇦⇦⇦⇦⇦

Basa Bali is a very melodic language, but the syllable stress and the pronunciation of some letters are somewhat strange to the English ear. Therefore please try to practice the Balinese words and phrases in this book together with a native speaker. I am sure a lot of *i anak Bali* will be eager to teach you the right pronunciation.

Stress

All the *kruna Bali* have to be stressed very clearly on the **last** syllable: sa**TE**; na**SI**; gu**RU**. Be careful when you mix *baSA BaLI* with Indonesian words, since many Indonesian speakers tend to place stress on the penultimate (next to last) syllable. By getting your stress right, you will be better understood in *BaLI!* Be**CIK** (OK)?

Vowels

a this vowel occurs at the beginning or middle of a word and is pronounced like **a** in r**a**ther: *tawang* know, *awinan* cause, *natah* yard, farm.

a similar to **o** in h**o**w, but a bit more open. This vowel occurs as the final sound of a word: *apa?* what? *ada* there is/are. The letter is also found in the prefixes *ka–*, *ma–*, and *pa–*: *majalan* to go by foot (from *jalan* way, trip). For this vowel especially you must listen to the pronunciation of a native speaker!

e short like **e** in le**tt**er but somewhat lighter like **i** in di**r**ty: *lembu* cow, *sekar* flower.

ê stressed like long **é** in pass**é**: *tekên* with, *dêwa* god (address or epithet). **ê** is usually written undifferentiated as a normal **e**.

i like **i** in Bal**i**: *dija?* where, *titiang* I. **i** in the last stressed syllable sounds sometimes similar to the short **e**: *inggih* (*inggéh*) yes, *saking* (*sakéng*) from.

o like **o** in g**o**: *topeng* mask, *portrêt* photo.

u like **oo** in t**oo**: *gumi* earth, *tulung* help.

The **a** is the most difficult letter of *basa Bali*, but it is the language's most characteristic tone, and it sounds quite lovely. To make things clearer for the reader, in this book **a** is distinguished from **a**, but the underlining does not occur in printed Balinese.

Two vowels together are usually pronounced separately, with no glottal stop. **aa** is pronounced **a–a**: *baan*. **ae** is pronounced **a–e** *mael* expensive. Only **au** is pronounced as a diphthong. It sounds like **o** in c**o**w, but a bit more open: *taur* pay.

Pronunciation Guide ⟡⟡⟡⟡⟡⟡⟡⟡⟡

Consonants

Basa Bali doesn't have the letters **f**, **q**, **v**, or **z** or the combination **th**. Most consonants are pronounced nearly the same as in English. The exceptions are as follows:

b or **d** found in the middle of a word after a consonant is very faint and hard to hear: *gambelan* (sounds like *gam'elan*), *gendis* (sounds like *gen'is*) sugar.

c is quite strong, like **ch** in **Ch**ina: *carik* paddy-field, *cicing* dog.

g hard like **g** in **g**oat: *gambelan*, *marga* road.

h 1) is silent at the beginning of a word, and is sometimes omitted: *halus* or *alus* refined, distinguished.

2) is quite distinctly voiced between two vowels: *kesugihan* property.

3) is a distinct glottal stop at the end of a word: *buah* fruit, betel, *mudah* cheap.

j is quite similar to **j** in **j**ungle, but it sounds, especially at the beginning of a word, a little bit more like **dy**: *jagi* will happen.

k 1) at the beginning and in the middle of a word is quite distinct, as **k** in **k**ey: *kopi* coffee, *makejang* all.

2) at the end of a word is more like a distinct vowel break (glottal stop): *nampek* near.

r is distinctly rolled like a Spanish or Russian r: **rer**a**ma** father and mother, *ca**ru*** offering to the nether world.

ng is very soft like **ng** in mi**ng**le. To pronounce **ng** correctly as an initial sound you have to give it some emphasis: **ng**udiang why, **ng**ud*a* young, **ng**eng feeling uneasy. Note that like Indonesian, in the combination **ngg** the second **g** is pronounced as a distinct letter: *ge**ngg**ong (ge**ng**–**g**ong)* Jew's–harp, *panga**nggo** (pangang–**g**o)* dress.

ny is like **ny** in la**ny**ard: *n**y**en?* who? *n**y**uh* coconut.

Notes on spelling

Originally *bas*a *Bali* was written with *aksar*a Balinese letters. Writing was done on *lontar*, dried palmleaf ribs, as well as depicted in paintings. Nowadays romanized spelling is found in the school books and elsewhere, although you will discover variations in use. The spelling of this book conforms to *Kamus Bali–Indonesia*, the most complete and authoritative dictionary of the Balinese language.

Sometimes the difficult **a** vowel will be written as **e**: for example, *ke* (to, for) instead of *k*a.

The Aksara Alphabet

ha	na	ca	ra	ka
da	ta	sa	wa	la
ma	ga	ba	nya	
pa	ja	ya	nya	

Pur<u>a</u> Sad<u>a</u>

Sekanan

✧ ✧ ✧ ✧ ✧ ✧ Different Language Levels

A butler speaking to his master will always select more refined words—he is "speaking upward." By contrast, his master, wanting to discuss the same subject, will choose more simple language—he is "down speaking." The *anak Bali* do the same thing. They may use either *alus*, refined words or more or less *kasar* rough, common words. *Ada umpama*—there is an example:

A farmer of low caste speaking to his friend is using *basa kasar*—as well as a high caste member speaking to a farmer concerning a low caste member:

Ia mara teka.   He just arrived.

A farmer speaking to or referring to a high class member or one high class member talking with another one is using *basa alus*:

Ida wawu rauh.   He just arrived.

But if the *ia* (he) is well known—perhaps his name is Made, than it is best to use his name:
*Made **wawu rauh** or Made mara teka.*

The meaning is quite the same, but the phrases are now in *basa Bali madia* (middle Balinese)—a mixture of high and low Balinese with a few words of its own. This is also called the polite language and it is very popular nowadays in Bali.

Do you think this is rather confusing? Maybe it is

Different Language Levels ✧ ✧ ✧ ✧ ✧ ✧

somewhat! But at the same time it is adventurous and interesting. Without knowing this facet of *basa Bali*, you would not really understand the traditional social structure of the *nusa*, island. Here the caste system is not at all based on rigid distinctions of occupational and dietary restrictions as in India. Instead, "caste" merely implies a common understanding of social status, expressed exclusively in these linguistic layers.

Some scholars distinguish five or even more levels of Balinese. Knowing this may be interesting from a scientific point of view, but it doesn't help at all if you want to have a practical conversation!

For our purposes we will assume there are only three levels. The everyday, low *basa kasar* is the basic level derived from the original old Balinese. The refined *basa alus* is a linguistic melting pot of Sanskrit, old Javanese, some Dutch and Indonesian, as well as old Balinese words. The language of this booklet will be the simple *basa kasar*, but some terms from *kruna alus* are included so that you might learn a practical *basa madia*.

Many words are the same for all language levels. There are only a determined number of terms which differ with language levels, mainly concerning human beings—what they are and what they do.

When and why should we speak everyday Balinese, *basa kasar*?

Theoretically we could speak only refined Balinese in order not to be objectionable to anyone. But not everybody can understand *basa alus*. In Buleleng, Northern Bali nearly all of the people speak quite *kasar*. In Southern Bali, if we speak with farmers using too many *kruna alus*, they may understand us, but they will have difficulty communicating with us. They will feel *lek ati* (ashamed or shy of heart), because they are struck by your "overdressed language" (Your newspaper seller would not feel very comfortable if you called her "My lady"!). People will accept you without frustration only when they perceive you are on the same basic *kasar* social level. Besides speaking their language you must not make them feel ashamed because you choose to use a very refined level of language! But on the other hand that doesn't mean you must avoid all *kruna alus*. On the contrary your language is considered quite polite, if you generally speak *kasar*, but often interject some *alus* expressions, for example:

inggih	yes, sure, right, isn't it? (the last syllable is pronounced very distinctly, with the second **i** pronounced more like the short and dull Balinese **e**)

19

Different Language Levels ⇦⇦⇦⇦⇦⇦

nenten, tan	no, not
patut	yes, sure, really
kênten	like this, so
napi?	what?
punapi?	why? in what way?
saking dija?	from where?
becik	good, beautiful

When and why should we speak refined *basa alus*?

So theoretically we could speak only *basa kasar* "upgraded" more or less—more to *basa madia* (middle language) or less to *basa biasa* ("normal" or average language). But there are three exceptions:

1. If you are speaking of very *alus* things—especially concerning *agama*, religion, you must use *kruna alus* throughout. Therefore, such terms will be found in this book.

2. If you are speaking to high caste people or, just as importantly, to high officials, it is better to use *kruna alus* for all terms concerning human beings. Only about seven or eight percent of *i anak Bali* are of the *triwangsa* (the three higher castes). But you need to keep in mind that many waitresses in *restoran*, restaurants and a lot of taxi drivers are *brahmana* (the first caste, to which belong all high priests) or *satria* (the second highest warrior caste).

When confronted with *basa kasar* they will become pale because of feeling **jengah** (the *alus* form of *lek*, meaning ashamed or angry). Therefore a conversation in a *restoran* in *basa alus* will be recorded in this booklet.

3. Balinese children and youth speaking to their parents tend to use *kruna alus* and avoid *kruna kasar*. When addressing their teachers and elders, they usually try to include as many *alus* words as possible.

All *kruna alus* in this book are printed in bold type.

Warung ⟡⟡⟡⟡⟡⟡⟡⟡⟡⟡ ⟡⟡⟡⟡⟡⟡

We start with a small talk at one of the *warung* (vending booth), the original Balinese information and conversation center. Even in the smallest hamlet you will find at least three or four such stalls. You can buy *kopi* (coffee), *biu* (banana), *jaja* (rice flour cake), *kacang* (peanuts), *sabun* (soap) and *wedang ane dingin* (Lit: Drinks which (are) cold). If you want to talk with the people, to find out when an **odalan**, temple festival is starting or what else is happening, the best way is to sit down at the *warung* and have a pot of *kopi* and, last but not least, a lot of time. There is no formal greeting phrase in *basa Bali*. You only have to sit down, smile and start talking:

Wenten wedang, pak/bu/gek?
Do you have hot coffee?
(Lit: Is there–coffee–hot, –father/mother/miss?)

Inggih—ad*a*!
Yes—there is!

Icen **tiang** *kopi* **panes** *misi gula/tusing misi gula.*
Give me coffee hot with sugar/without sugar

*Bap*a *(pak) nyak biu wiadin jaja?*
Do you want banana or cake?

(Lit: Father–like–banana–or–cake?)

Yen ada **tiang** *ngidih kacang.*
If there are I beg for nuts.

Inggih, wenten *kacang* **sanê becik** *pisan.*
Yes, there are nuts that very good.
(Lit: Good–very much).
Kacang-e aji-ne aji kuda?
How much are the nuts?
(Lit: Nuts–their–price–their–price–how much?)

Aji satus (rupiah).
They cost 100 rupiah.
(Lit: Price–100).

Idih buin kopi.
May I have more coffee, please.
(Lit: Beg–more–coffee).

The best way to catch a feeling for the *kruna Bali*
is to learn these examples by heart.

Forms of Address ⇦⇦⇦⇦⇦⇦⇦⇦⇦⇦

Given the different language levels, it is very important that foreigners use the proper forms of address toward Balinese. These forms of address have the same function as pronouns in European languages. By using the wrong word for "you" or "I," you are almost sure to offend someone from the start! Note in particular the everyday (*madia*) and the refined (*alus*) way of addressing someone. Remember, when talking to someone of high social status (or at least you think so), you will need to use the *alus* terms.

	Everyday Balinese	High Balinese
I	*tiang*	**titiang**
we	*i raga makejang* (Lit: The body –all)	**timpal-timpal/ titiangê/ semeton titiangê** (Lit: My friends/ my brothers-sisters)
you (s.)	*raganê*	**jero**
you (pl.)	*nyama makejang*	**semeton sami**
he/she/it	*ia*	**ipun/ida**
they	*danê*	**ida**

Notes:

First person plural: *i raga makejang* includes the person addressed (Indonesian: *kita*). *I raga* may be used if the person addressed is excluded (Indonesian: *kami*).

Second person ("you"): Some rules for addressing people are as follows.

1. **Jero**—for persons you do not yet know well or whom you are meeting for the first time. (**Jero**=inside, insider, an expression of respect.)

2. Address people according to their age:
Pak/Bapą/Pak guru (Indonesian: father/father–teacher)—for man
Aji (Triwangsa)—for nobleman
Buk/Mêmê (mother)—for woman
Biyang—for women of Triwangsa castes
Pekak (grandfather)—for elderly man
Dadong (grandmother)—for elderly woman
Gus—for young man or boy
Gêg (young maiden, pretty one)—for young woman or girl

3. Use *Pak* or *Buk* plus the name of the addressed, once you have been introduced. You may also use the name only, if you would like to be more informal.

4. *Raganê* should only be used to address a child or a close friend. If in doubt, use **Jero**, *Pak* or *Bu* for "you."

Third person: It is also common to use *bapą* (father) for "he," *mêmê* (mother) for "she" and *ene/**puniki*** (this) or *ento/**punikạ*** (that) for "it."

Grammar I ✧✧✧✧✧✧✧✧✧✧✧✧✧✧✧

The grammar of *basa Bali* is not so complex, but there are some basic rules you must know.

WORD ORDER IN THE SENTENCE

Balinese sentences follow a regular word order (syntax): **subject—verb—object**, which is similar to English.

Bapa rauh sakeng Bangli. Bapa teka uli Bangli.
Father comes to Bangli. Father comes from Bangli.

A noun followed by an adjective will be understood as a complete sentence, and if you raise your voice, a question:

*Kopine **panes**.*
The coffee (is) hot.

*Kopine **panes**?*
Is the coffee hot?

Biune nasak.
The banana (is) ripe.

Punyan-punyan nyuh tegeh.
The coconut trees are high.
(Lit: Tree–tree–coconut–high.)

NOUNS

Nouns and adjectives have no endings for case and number.

Possession

The pronoun or noun after its subject indicates possession:

warung tiang	my stall
*gambar **titiang***	my painting
*barang pak/buk/**jero***	your package
*satua pak/buk/**jero***	his/her story

Possession can be indicated more clearly by adding the suffixe –ne (Indonesian –nya) to the word, meaning "his," "her," "its" or "of":

pianak gurunê	(the) teacher's child
warung dadongnê	grandmother's stall
titinê	the path, his bridge
	(*titi*=path, small bridge)
saput warnanê	the color of the cloth
	(*warna*=color)

In all these cases –ne added to the word indicates possession. When followed by another noun or adjective, often a noun ending in a vowel will add the ending –n:

bungan **padma** / *bunganê* **padma**	the lotus flower
	(*bunga*=flower)
bunganê apa? apa bunganê	what flower?
wastan titiangê	my name (**wasta**=name)
(also: **titiang mawasta**	I am named)

Plural

Plural is expressed mainly by context:

Tiang *ngidih kacang.*
May I have nuts, please? (Lit: I–request–nut.)
It is obvious that you want more than one nut!

Mêmê ngelah bêbêk liu.
You have many ducks.
(Lit: Mother–possess–ducks–many.)

Here the word *liu*, many, expresses the fact that *mêmê* has more than one *bêbêk*.

Reduplication of the noun means "a variety of" and only rarely indicates the plural: *kruna-kruna* words, *pura-pura* temples, but **sami puranê ring Bali** all the temples in Bali.

Grammar I ⇦ ⇦ ⇦ ⇦ ⇦ ⇦ ⇦ ⇦ ⇦ ⇦ ⇦ ⇦ ⇦ ⇦

To denote a group of persons, *para* is often used: *para pedanda* the group of priests, *para ksatria* the class of rulers and warriors.

Gender
For the most part, Balinese does not differentiate nouns by gender. Only a few terms of Sanskrit origin have both a male and a female form:

putri	daughter
putra	son
dewi	goddess
dewa	god
raksasi	demonic giantess
raksasa	demonic giant/stone guard figure before temple gates
dedari, widiadari	heavenly nymph
widiadara	Adonis, handsome youth

(If you see a very fascinating girl, with angel-like wings, taking a bath in a lake or a river, you can be sure, that's a **widiadari**. The nymphs are shown on many paintings and stone carvings and there is an interesting **dedari** trance dance as well!)

If you want to denote gender you may place *muani/lanang* male or *luh/wadon* female behind the word: *siap muani* rooster, *siap luh* hen.

ARTICLES
No definite article "the" is needed in Balinese, although it may be expressed by –*e* (his, her, their) added to the final consonant:

kacange the nut, *warunge* the stall, *odalane* the temple festival

28

or –*ne* added to the final vowel:
jajane the cake, *biune* the banana, *mêmêne* the mother,
bapane the father.

(Note: Stress will fall on the article as the last syllable. An
article added to final **a** changes it to **a**.)

For persons, the article *i* (pronounced like **i** in k**i**ng) is
used before the word:
i mêmê the mother, *i bapa* the father

There is no indefinite article "a" or "an," although if you
need to express it, you may use the numeral *a*, "one":
dina day, *dinane* the day, *a dina* (or *adina*) one day.

ADJECTIVES
The adjective always follows the noun:

*Ada kopi **panes**?*
Do you have hot coffee?
(Lit: There is–coffee–hot?)

***Tiang** ngidih biu nasak.*
May I have a ripe banana.
(Lit: I–request–banana–ripe.)

Mêmê ngelah bêbêk gede.
She has a big duck.
(Lit: Mother–possess–duck–big.)

In Balinese any noun can be used as an adjective.
Generally speaking, there is no difference between nouns
and adjectives in *basanê Bali*.

Ada gelang slaka.
There is a silver bracelet.
(Lit: There is–bracelet–silver.)

Grammar I ⇦⇦⇦⇦⇦⇦⇦⇦⇦⇦⇦⇦⇦

Togoge kayu nangka.
The statue is made of jackfruit wood
(Lit: Statue–the–wood–jackfruit.)

But: *Nangkanê aji kayu.*
The jackfruit (carving) is made from wood. (*aji* has many different meanings: made from, price, father, teacher.)

Placement of adjectives of quantity

The adjectives of quantity *akeh* (much) and *bedik* (few) follow the general rule of adjective following the noun it modifies. However, the adjectives *liu/**akêh*** (much or many) and *bedik, abedik/**akedik*** (few) as well as numbers are often placed before the verbs *gelah, ngelah* (to have, possess, belong to) and *ada*:

Bapa ngelah panak papat or *Panakne Bapa ada patpat.*
He (father) has four children.
(Lit: Father–four–has–children.)

Mêmê liu ngelah bêbêk.
She (mother) has many ducks.
(Lit: Mother–many–possess–duck.)

Comparison

Adjectives can be changed to the comparative (the –er ending in English) by the addition of *–an* or *–nan*, and to the superlative (–est) by using the adverb *paling* (most):

Adjective	Comparative	Superlative
melah	*melahan*	*paling melah*
becik	**becikan**	**paling becik**
good	better	best
jegêg	*jegêgan*	*paling jegêg*

ayu	**ayuan**	*paling ayu*
beautiful (nice)	more beautiful	most beautiful
liu	*liunan*	*paling liu*
akêh	**akêhan**	**paling akêh**
much/many	more	most
gedê	*gedênan*	*paling gedê*
ageng	**agengan**	**paling ageng**
big (great)	bigger	biggest
	(greater)	(greatest)
cerik/cenik	*cerikan*	*paling cerik*
alit	**alitan**	**paling alit**
small	smaller	smallest

Paribasa (a proverb):
Liunan krebeg, kuangan ujan.
More thunder, less rain.
(Said of someone who says much but does little, like the saying "His bark is worse than his bite.")

The thing to which comparison is made follows the word *padaang tekên*/**banding ring** ("than," "compared to"):

Everyday Balinese: *Punyan nyuh tegehan padaang teken punyan biu.*
High Balinese: **Wit klapa agengan banding ring wit pisang**.
The coconut tree is taller than the banana tree.

"Too, excessive" is expressed by the comparative or *bas/bes* placed before the word:
liunan or *bes liu*   too much
cenikan or *bes cenik*   too small

"Very" may be expressed by the superlative or *pesan* placed behind the word:

Grammar I ✧✧✧✧✧✧✧✧✧ ✧✧✧✧✧✧

paling tegeh or *tegeh pesan*   very high, tall
paling jegêg or *jegêg pesan*   very beautiful

Pada . . . tekên (same . . . as) or *pada . . . -ne* are used to express equality:

Punyan nyuh pada tegehnê tekên punyan rontal
The coconut tree is as tall as the lontar tree.

Umahê di dêsa enê makejang pada gedênê
The houses in this village are all the same size.
(Lit: Houses–the–in–village–this–all–same–size– their.)

In Balinese, most adjectives can also function as adverbs.

VERBS

There are no verb endings in Balinese. However, there are verb prefixes.

The verb "to be"

"To be" is generally omitted in *basane Bali*. You may use *ene/**puniki*** this, these, this is, these are, to express "to be." A similar expression is *ento/**punika*** that, that is, those are.

Nyuh jaen pesan.
The coconuts are very delicious.
(Lit: Coconut–delicious–very much.)

Nyuhe jaen pesan.
The coconut is very delicious.

kasar:	*Nyuh enê jaen pesan.*
alus:	***Klapa puniki** jaen **pisan**.*
	This coconut is delicious
	(Lit: Coconut–this–delicious–
	very much.)

kasar:	*Nyuh ento jaen pesan.*
alus:	***Klapa punika** jaen **pisan**.*
	That coconut is very delicious.

But: *Bojogê demen tekên nyuh enê.*
The monkey likes this coconut.

Tiang demen nangkanê uli desa ento.
I (would) like the jackfruit from that village.

Grammar II ◇◇◇◇◇◇◇◇◇◇ ◇◇◇◇◇◇

Other common verbs

ada/**wênten**	there is, there are, have
dadi/**dados**	become, be able, may, be allowed
demen/**seneng**	like, love
lakar/**pacang**, **jagi**	shall, will, want, desire
luas/**lunga**	go, come, depart
teka/**rauh**	come, arrive
tawang/**uning**	know
tepukin/**cingakin**	see, look

kasar: *Di warung ene ada biu.*
alus: ***Ring** warung **puniki wênten pisang.***
In this stall there are bananas.

kasar: *Ada biu dini?*
alus: ***Wênten pisang driki?***
Are there bananas here?

Ada sarung di toko enê?
Can one get sarongs in this shop?
(Lit: Are there–sarong–in–shop–this?)

*Ada kopi **panes**?*
Do you have hot coffee?
(Lit: Is there–coffee–hot?)

***Inggih**, ada!*
Yes, there is!

Mêmê adа jajа anê jaen.
Mother has cake which is delicious.
(*ane* (Indonesian: *yang*)=that, which or who)

Dalang adа wayang kulit anê becik.
The puppeteer has shadow play figures that are beautiful.

Tiang adа buku anê anyar.
I have a book that is new.

I guru dadi tukang gambar.
The teacher becomes a painter.
(*tukang*=craftsman, master of)

Nuju rahinа Saraswati tan dados macа sastra.
During the (feast) day of Saraswati it is forbidden to read books.

Verb prefixes

Several common verbs are regularly used in their root form without alteration. That is easy. But most other verbs are modified with prefixes and suffixes. The following is an *umpama/upama, upami* example:

The root word for "give" is *baang*. The root form is used in the imperative:
Baang i mêmê jajа!
Give her the sweets!
(Lit: Give–the–mother–sweets!)

Grammar II ✧ ✧ ✧ ✧ ✧ ✧ ✧ ✧ ✧ ✧ ✧ ✧ ✧

But in an assertion or question, the prefix *nge–* is added. Moreover, for the sake of euphony the initial **b** becomes **m**, so that the root *baang* becomes *nge-maang*:

Tiang ngemaang i mêmê jaja.
I give her sweets.

Bapa ngemaang i mêmê jaja / Bapa maang i mêmê jaja.
Father gives the mother sweets.

Apa Bapa maang i meme jaja?
Are you giving her sweets?
(Lit: Father–give–mother–sweets?)

In *basane Bali* many transitive verbs are formed by adding *nge–* to a noun or adjective. This is why the prefix *nge–* is necessary. Moreover, intransitive verbs are formed by adding the prefix *ma–* to a noun:

Jalan way, path; *majalan* to go, travel.

In this book the root form is placed in parentheses behind the prefixed word, when it is *patut* (appropriate, important) to know it: *ngemaang* (*baang*).
If the root of a verb is a noun, the English translation will also be given: *majalan* (*jalan* way, travel).
The prefixed form will be given after the root form: *idih*, *ngidih* request, ask for.

Do not be too surprised when confronted with a very strange sounding prefixed word. In time, you will learn to recognize the basic root word. Here are some examples of prefixes:

dagingipun	contents, meat
madaging	filled with, containing, with
nagingin	to fill (affix *n– –in*)
takon, matakon	to ask
patakon	question
saut/saur	answer
masaut/masaur	to answer
pasaut/pasaur	(the) answer
adanê	name
madan	to be called
ngadanin	to call, to name

Paribasa (a proverb)

Buka goake ngadanin ibanê.
Like the crow calling its own name.
(Said of a person who boasts about cheating others.)

Passive voice

Omit the prefix for verbs in the passive voice:

Active voice: *Mêmê ngidih kacang tekên tiang.*
She requests nuts from me.

Grammar II ⇦ ⇦ ⇦ ⇦ ⇦ ⇦ ⇦ ⇦ ⇦ ⇦ ⇦ ⇦ ⇦

Passive voice: *Kacang idiha baan mêmê tekên tiang.*
Nuts are requested by her from me.

Active voice: *I bapa liu ngelah pipis.*
He has much money.
(Lit: The–father–much–has–money; *liu*, much.)

Passive voice: *Pipis liu gelah i bapa.*
Much money belongs to him.

Active voice: *Akuda bapa ngelah panak?*
You have how many children?
(Lit: How many–father–possess–children?)

Passive voice: *Akuda panak gelah bapa?*
How many children do you have?

Active voice: *Anak luh ngidih jaja.*
The girl (Lit: Child–female) asks for sweets

Passive voice: *Jaja idiha baan anak luh.*
Sweets are requested by the girl.

Tense

Balinese verbs show no tense. "Arrived," "arrive" and "will arrive" are all translated as *teka*. However, many words are used to express time present, past and future. As in English, these words are placed before the main verb.

Present tense: Most sentences are assumed to be in the present tense. Use *jani/**mangkin*** (now) to emphasize that something is happening at this very moment:

Mêmê tusing ngelah bêbêk.
She does not have any ducks.

I anak cenik manjus.
The small child is taking a bath (*manjus*=bathe, take a bath).

Tiang jani teka di Singaraja.
I am now arriving in Singaraja.

Tiang jani majalan ka Tirtagangga.
I am now walking to Tirtagangga.

Past tense: Use *mara/***wawu*** (just now), *dibi/***ring dibi*** (yesterday), *suba/***sampun*** (already, once), *suba maan* (already has been) and *tondên/* ***durung*** (not yet):

Tiang mara teka di Singaraja.
I just arrived in Singaraja.

Dibi bapa makaad uli Bali.
Yesterday he departed from Bali.

Suba ada poh nasak.
The mango is already ripe.

Tiang suba maan ka Ubud.
I have been to Ubud once.

Mêmê tondên ada bêbêk.
She did not yet have any ducks.
(Lit: Mother–not yet have–possess–duck.)

Grammar II ✧✧✧✧✧✧✧✧ ✧✧✧✧✧✧

Future tense: Use *lakar/**pacang*** (will, shall), *nyak/**kayun*** (want, desire), *buin mani/**bênjang*** (tomorrow), and *akejep/**ajebos*** (at once):

Lakar lunga.
(I) shall go.

I anak cenik nyak manjus.
The small child wants to bathe.

Buin mani mêmê lakar ka peken.
Tomorrow she will go to the market.

⇨ ⇨ ⇨ ⇨ ⇨ ⇨ ⇨ **Questions and Requests**

There are three ways to express a question:

1. For most questions you may simply raise your voice toward the end of the sentence:

Bapa bisa basa Bali?
Do you know the Balinese language?

2. You may add the suffix *–ke* to the first word in the sentence, which is its "topic" or main idea:

Bapakê bisa basa Bali?
Are you the one who knows Balinese?

Bisa bapa basa Bali?
Do you *know* Balinese?

3. You may use a question word:

kasar	alus	English
apa?	**napi?**	what?
nyên?	**sira?**	who?
engkên?	**encên**	what? which? which one?
ane encên?	**sane encên?**	which one?
kuda?	**aji kuda**	how much? how many?
dija?	**ring dija?**	where?
kija?	**lunga kija?**	where to?
uli dija?	**saking napi**	where from?
nguda?	**ngudiang?**	why?

Questions and Requests ◇ ◇ ◇ ◇ ◇ ◇ ◇

apakrana?	**punapi awinan?**	why?
kênkên?	**sapunapi?**	how?
pidan?	**ring pidan?**	when? (past)
buin pidan?	**malih pidan?**	when? (future)
nyên adanê?	**sira wastanê?**	What's (your, his, her) name?
apa orta?	**napi gatranê?**	What's new? (How are you?)
kuda?	**aji kuda**	How much?
lakar kija?	**lunga kija?**	Where are (you) going?
apa ento?	**napi punika?**	What's that?
pukul kuda jani?	**pukul kuda mangkin?**	What time is it?
lakar nguda kema?	**pacang ngudiang merika?**	Why do you want to go there also?

How do you address somebody you meet on the street? When is it better to speak simple *kasar*, and when are we obliged to talk in a more refined *alus* way?

Sometimes you can guess a person's social position. You see a man wearing a white shirt and a big watch, and perhaps dark eyeglasses. His fingernails are about three cm long. You can be sure he's a *guru*. He may or may not be from a higher caste, but what teacher would not, in the bottom of his heart, want to be more highly esteemed? So it would better to start by addressing him with as many *alus* words as possible. His class rank and family background will be expressed in his name. (This is why *i anak Bali* try to find out the name of anyone they meet very quickly.) Then, once you have some familiarity with the person and his background, you will know whether to continue the conversation in *alus* or *biasa* Balinese.

There is no standard greeting in *basa Bali*. People meeting you for the first time might begin the conversation by asking your name:

Sira wastan jeronê? *(kasar: Nyên adanê?)*
What's your name?
(Lit: Who–name–the–esteemed–the?)

*Adan **titiangê**/tiang madan Guntur—**inggih**. Sira*

Small Talk ✧✧✧✧✧✧✧✧ ✧✧✧✧✧✧

wastan bapanê?
My name is Günter, indeed. What is your name?

Tiang Ketut.
I (am) Ketut.

So, now we both are informed that we are quite simple people. I can see it from his name (see the chapter on names and rank) and because he continues to use *basa biasa*. The conversation might continue as follows:

Guntur uli negara dija?
Guntur is from which country? (Lit: Country where? *negara*=country)

or: *Uli dija?* (alus: ***Saking (pu)napi?***)
Where are you from? (i.e. Where is your home?)

Tiang uli negara Eropa/Amerika, ***inggih.***
I (am) from Europe/America, indeed.

Mara teka uli dija? or *Uli dija?* (alus: ***Ring dija?***)
(You) just came from where?

Tiang mara teka uli Ubud.
I just came from Ubud.

Indeng-indeng!
(Just) turning round! (A shure way to get a laugh!)

(Lit.: Go there and here)

Once you've been asked your name and where

you're from, inevitably you'll be asked about your family and marital status:

Bapa suba makurenan?
Are you already married? (*kuren* family, *makurenan* married, *kurenan* wife, husband).

Inggih. *Tiang suba ngantên.*
Yes. I am already married (*antên* groom/bride (*ngantên* marry, married).

Kurenan bapanê dija jani?
Where is you wife now?
(Lit: Partner–of–father–now–where?)

Ia jani di Ubud, di losmen.
She is now in Ubud, in the lodge.

Akuda bapa ngelah pianak?
How many children do you have?
(Lit: How many–father–has–children?)

Dadua—*abesik luh, abesik muani.*
Two—one female and one male.

Becik pisan—*duang panak genep!*
Very good—two children are enough! (A reference to the Indonesian birth control policy: *Dua anak cukup!*)

Such is the sort of conversation you might expect in Bali. *Makejang anak Bali*—everybody in Bali—as soon as he or she knows your name, will be interested in knowing about your family. Please consult the glossaries to find some kinship terms. Some are the same for both females and males, evidence that gender differences are not very prominent in Balinese society, as well linguistical as in real life!

	kasar	*alus*
family	nyama-braya	**semetonan, kulawarga**
husband	kurenan	**suami**
wife	kurenan	**rabi**
bride/groom	pangantênan	
marry, married	makurenan	**marabian**
child	panak	**oka**
daughter	pianak luh	**oka istri**
son	pianak muani	**putra**
brother	nyama	**semeton**
brother (older)	beli	**raka**
brother (younger)	adi muani	**ari lanang**
sister	nyama	**semeton sanê istri**
sister (older)	mbok	**raka**
sister (younger)	adi luh	**ari/rai**
father	bapa	**aji**
mother	mêmê	**biyang, ibu**

parents	*mêmê bapa*	**rerama**
grandfather	*pekak, kak*	**kakiang**
grandmother	*dadong*	**nini**
grandchild	*cucu*	**putu**
aunt	*uwa*	**bibi**
uncle	*uwa/wa*	**paman**
female	*luh*	**wadon**
male	*muani*	**lanang**

When you are about to leave, you will be asked:

*Bapa/Mêmê lakar lunga kija? (alus: **Lunga kija?**)*
Where do you want to go?

Tiang lakar ka Singakerta.
I want to go to Singakerta.

Tusing ada bêmo ka Singakerta uli dini.
There is no bemo to Singakerta from here.

Guntur tan demen nyêwa montor?
You don't want to hire a car?

*Tusing demen negakin montor, krana nyêwa montor
mael pesan.*
I don't want to ride a car, because to hire a car (is)
very expensive.

Sing kênkên. Tiang demen majalan.
No problem. I want to walk.

When taking leave, to say "thank you," some

Small Talk ✧✧✧✧✧✧✧✧ ✧✧✧✧✧✧✧

Balinese will say:
Matur suksma. Thank you very much.

But this expression is a direct translation from the Indonesian, and is used only in *basa alus*. Originally *basa Bali* had no way of expressing thanks. So not all *anak Bali* will understand this new Balinese formula. Therefore with people speaking everyday Balinese, you'd better simply use the Indonesian *"terima kasih."*

To express "you are welcome" you say:
Inggih! or *Sama-sama!* (Lit: the same for you)

When the Balinese leave their parents, some friends, a teacher, a party or the shrine of a god and so forth, saying goodbye is very important. Very characteristically, the Balinese will always beg for permission to leave:
Tiang **pamit.**　　　　　 Excuse me.

And the answer naturally will be:
Inggih, rarisang mamargi!
Fine, please go your way!

Paribasa (a proverb):
Gagah sepêda kembung baan angin.
As a bike blown up with wind.
(Somebody who likes to boast very much, but there is nothing behind it.)

95% of Bali's population consists of rice farmers, the lowest *sudra* or *jaba* caste. You will uniformly find that the Balinese are addressed according to their order of birth in the family:

Wayan	child No. 1 or *Putu*
Madê	child No. 2 or *Nengah/Kadêk*
Nyoman	child No. 3 or *Komang*
Ketut	child No. 4
Wayan	child No. 5 etc.

You can see that the Balinese expect to have large families! The names are the same for girls and boys. As an indicator of gender *I* is used for males and *Ni* for females.

Ni Wayan	first born child (female)
I Madê	second born child (male)

People of the rice farmer class will also have a second name. Their houses are called *umah*.

The names of *triwangsa*—high class people are:

1. *brahmana* highest caste of priests

Ida Bagus or **Bagus**	good one (male)
Ida Ayu or **Dayu**	beautiful one (female; **ayu**=beautiful)

Their houses are called **gria**.

Names and Rank ⇦ ⇦ ⇦ ⇦ ⇦ ⇦ ⇦ ⇦ ⇦ ⇦ ⇦ ⇦

2. *ksatria* second caste of soldiers and warriors
Anak Agung, **Agung**, **Dêwa** for men
(great man, great god; **Agung**=great, majestic)

Anak Agung, **Agung**, **Dêwi**, **Dêwayu** for women
(great woman, great, goddess, beautiful goddess).

Cokorda, **Dêwa Agung** for members of the king-
dom's ruling clan (**Cokorda**=honored foot, a reference to the abased position of the person addressing him)

Members of this caste tend to have the following
second names as well:

Raka	older sister/brother
Oka	child (**Anak Agung Oka**)
Rai	younger sister/brother
Anom	young woman
Ngurah	a name that indicates authority

Their houses are called **puri**.

3. *wesia* third caste of merchants and officials

Gusti	(lord) for men or women
Dêwa	for men
Dêsak	for women

Their houses are called **jero**.

Names of women of the rice farmer's caste who
marry a **triwangsa**: **jero istri**, **jero** luh.

⇨ ⇨ ⇨ ⇨ ⇨ ⇨ ⇨ ⇨ ⇨ ⇨ ⇨ ⇨ **Names and Rank**

Names of children of a **_triwangsa_** father and a rice
farmer's caste mother: **_Dêwa_** _Wayan_ (_Dêwayan_),
Dêwa _Madê_, etc. (For girls **_Dêwi_** _Wayan_, etc.)

Triwangsa will also have a second name denoting
their residence.

In the Restaurant ⟸⟸⟸⟸⟸ ⟸⟸⟸⟸⟸

If you are very fond of suckling pig, you must visit
the *warung* of the Gianyar *peken*. The bigger
restoran in Bali are run by the *triwangsa* class. The
following conversation is held in both *basa alus* and
basa biasa:

Wênten ajengan Bali sanê tulén?
Ada ajengan Bali anê tulén?
Do you have native Balinese dishes?
(Lit: Is there–meal–Bali–which–authentic?)

Wênten—inggih!
Ada—inggih!
We have, indeed!

Ajengan napi sanê wênten?
Ajengan *apa ada?*
Which dishes are they?
(Lit: Meal–what–is there?)

Wênten bê guling miwah bêbêk bêtutu.
Ada be guling muah bêbêk betutu.
There is roast pork and steamed duck.

Icên titiang bêbêk bêtutu.
Icên tiang bêbêk bêtutu.
Give me steamed duck (prepared with chopped
spices).

Inggih—Jero pacang nginum napi?
Inggih—*bapa lakar minum napi?*

Certainly. What would you like to drink, Sir?

Icên titiang wêdang têh tan medaging gendis.

Têh sing misi gula.

Give me hot tea without sugar.

(Lit: Give–me–hot drink–tea–not–containing– sugar.)

Jero uning basa Bali?

Bapa bisa basa Bali?

You know the Balinese language, Sir?

Titiang pacang melajah basa Bali. Sira wastan jeronê?

*Tiang lakar melajah basa Bali. Nyên adan **Jero**nê?*

I want to learn the Balinese language. May I ask your name, Ma'am? (Lit: Who–name–you–of?)

Wastan titiangê Dêwi.

Tiang madan Dêwi.

My name is Dêwi.

Titiang mawasta Guntur, inggih.

*Tiang madan Guntur, **inggih**!*

I am named Günter, much obliged.

Guntur sering-sering ring Bali?

Guntur sai-sai di Bali?

Are you often in Bali, Günter?

Titiang sampun ping tiga ring Bali.

Tiang suba ping telu di Bali.

This is my third time in Bali.

In the Restaurant ✧✧✧✧✧ ✧✧✧✧✧

After the meal:
Titiang pacang naur.
Tiang lakar mayah.
I would like to pay.

kasar	alus	English
mayah (bayah)	**naur (taur)**	pay
sai-sai	**sering–sering**	(very) often
ping telu	**ping tiga**	three times
makelo	**sué**	long time
peken	**pasar**	market

In every kitchen (*paon/***prantenan** or **pawaregan,** the kitchen of a **pura**) there are *basa gedê* (big spices). The basic meaning of *basa* is "tongue," and so by derivation the term can either mean "language," or, in cooking, "spices," and by extension, "chest of spices." From these spices is made *sambel*—a spicy sidedish included in the staple *nasi masambel* (boiled rice containing *sambel*), which is served three times a day.

Special Balinese meals are prepared for the *odalan* temple festivals. You may find such native repasts in Balinese *restoran* catering to the *tamiu*, guests from abroad. The dishes include:

godoh	fried banana
guling cêlêng (bê guling)	suckling pig
jukut urab	mixed vegetable with grated coconut
lawar	shredded coconut and spices mixed with minced meat
nasi bira	yellow rice with spices
satê, sasatê	barbecued small pieces of meat on skewers
soto babad	tripe soup (much more delicious than it sounds!)
ulam pêêsan	roasted fish and spices wrapped in banana leaf
urutan cêlêng	spicy pork sausages (available at special *warung*)

Numbers ✧ ✧ ✧ ✧ ✧ ✧ ✧ ✧ ✧ ✧ ✧ ✧ ✧ ✧ ✧

In Bali we will find ourselves counting things like *rupiah* (Indonesian currency), *mêtêr*, *kilo*, *biu*/**pisang** (bananas) or perhaps *siap*/**ayam** (chickens) or something like that. Borrowing from Javanese, Balinese numbers have quite a few unexpected forms.

The forms of the first seven numbers used in counting differ from the basic numbers, usually by adding *–ng*. Since it is especially common to encounter the *alus* forms for one, two and three, these are also given here.

	Basic Number	Counting Number	*alus*
1	*besik, siki*	siki, a-	**sa**
2	*dua*	duang	**kalih**
3	*telu*	telung	**tigang**
4	*pat*	petang	
5	*lima*	limang	
6	*nem, enam*	nem	
7	*pitu*	pitung	
8	*kutus*	kutus	
9	*sia*	sia	
10	*dasa*	dasa	

aukud siap/**aukud ayam** one chicken
duang ukud siap/**kalih ukud ayam** two chickens

Ukud is an example of a classifier word. When

counting, most nouns will take a particular classifier word, for example:

bulih for oblong fruits, stalks:

biu telung bulih	three bananas

bungkul for round objects and buildings:

nyuh kutus bungkul	eight coconuts
jineng abungkul	one rice barn

diri for persons:

anak Jawa limang diri	five Javanese

puun (from *punyan*=tree) for trees:

punyan nyuh duang puun	two coconut trees

ukud (derived from *ikuh*=tail) for animals:

siap muani petang ukud	four roosters

The numbers from 11 to 30 are also highly irregular, and must simply be memorized:

11	*solas*	21	*selikur*
12	*roras*	22	*dualikur*
13	*telulas*	23	*telulikur*
14	*patbelas*	24	*patlikur*
15	*limolas*	25	*selae*
16	*nembelas*	26	*nemlikur*
17	*pitulas*	27	*pitulikur*
18	*pelekutus*	28	*ululikur*
19	*siangolas*	29	*sangalikur*
20	*duang dasa*	30	*telung dasa*

Numbers ⟵⟵⟵⟵⟵⟵⟵⟵⟵⟵ ⟵⟵⟵⟵⟵

For numbers over 30, use the basic form for 1 to 9
for the last digit. However, there are special forms
for the numbers 35, 45 and 75. Note also the special
forms for 50, 80 and 90.

30	*telung dasa*	60	*nem dasa*
31	*telung dasa besik*	70	*pitung dasa*
32	*telung dasa dua*, etc.	75	*telung benang*
35	*pasasur*	80	*ulung dasa*
40	*petang dasa*	90	*sangang dasa* or
45	*setiman*		*sia dasa*
50	*sêket*		

For numbers over 100 the last two digits are indicated at the end. But even here there are some
unusual forms:

100	*satus*	1,111	*siu satus solas*
101	*satus besik*, etc.	1,200	*nem bangsit*
150	*karobelah*	1,400	*pitung bangsit*
175	*lebak*	2,000	*duang tali*
200	*satak*	3,000	*telung tali*
300	*telung atus*	4,000	*petang tali*
400	*samas*	5,000	*limang tali*
500	*limang atus*	6,000	*nem tali*
600	*telung atak*	7,000	*pitung tali*
700	*pitung atus*	8,000	*kutus tali*
800	*domas*	9,000	*sangang tali*
900	*sanga*	10,000	*alaksa*
1,000	*siu*	20,000	*duang laksa*

Because of the irregularities it would be best to learn all the *nomer* by heart. This can be quite mind-boggling!

For the numbers 1 to 10 there is a slightly different form used only in a *pasaut* (answer) to a question (*patakon*). Although you will not use them often, you need to recognize them when used:

1	*abesik*
2	*dadua, kakalih*
3	*tetelu, tetiga*
4	*patpat*
5	*lelima*
6	*nemnem*
7	*pepitu*
8	*akutus*
9	*asia*
10	*adasa*

Question: *Biu kuda? Telu wiadin nem?*
How many bananas are there, three or six?

Answer: *Nemnem!*   Six!

ITUNGAN calculation

lima	**pitu**	**pat**	**sia**	**nem**	**roras**
5	+ 7	- 4	x 9	/ 6	= 12
jangin	**juangin**	**pang**	**bagi**	**pada**	**têkên**
(teken)	(kuangin)	(ping)	(pah)		

Market Day   ⇔ ⇔ ⇔ ⇔ ⇔ ⇔ ⇔ ⇔ ⇔ ⇔ ⇔ ⇔ ⇔

In the towns of Bali, *pekenan*—market day—is held
once every three days.

Dibi ada pekenan di Sukawati.
Yesterday was market day in Sukawati.

Nuju dina Pekenan di Ubud.
Today it's market day in Ubud.

Timpal-timpal muah tiang luas ka peken.
(My) friends and I are going to the market.

Wênten *manas?*
Do you have pineapple?

Aksama tiang—tusing wênten. **Jero** *kayun biu?*
Kayun markisa?
Pardon me—there are none. Do you want bananas?
Passion fruit?

Sing demen. **Wênten** *salak—inggih! Jaen enê?*
I don't want that. You have *salak*, I see! Are they
delicious?

Salak enê manis. Kayun?
This *salak* is sweet. (Do you) want (any)?

Akilo ajinê kuda?
How much does one kilo cost?
(Lit: One–kilo–its–price–how much?)

Telung tali!
Three thousand rupiah!

Telung tali? Mael pesan ajinê! Baang limang atus!

Three thousand? Too expensive! (I'll) give 500!
(*mael*=expensive)

*Aduh pocol-pocol! Salak ajinê tigang tali rupiah! Enê
suba mudah!*

My goodness, I'll lose money! The price of *salak* is
three thousand rupiah! This is already cheap!
(*mudah*=inexpensive, cheap)

Jero dadi kuangin ajinê abedik?
Can you lower its price a little?

Duang tali limang atus bisa!
Two thousand five hundred is possible!

Lakar bayah tiang siu limang atus !
I will pay one thousand five hundred!

Sing bisa. Tekên jero aji mati duang tali!
Not possible. For you my best price is two thousand!
(*aji mati*="death price," lowest price)

Mirip matemu di tengah! Duang tali—inggih?
Perhaps we meet in the middle! Two thousand—
agreed?

Inggih—adung! Buin wênten nangka. Jero kayun?
Yes, agreed! Still, there is jackfruit. Do you want
any?

Mirib buin–mani!
Perhaps tomorrow!

Market Day   ✧✧✧✧✧✧✧✧✧✧✧✧✧

*pipis/**jinah***	money
*nyandang/**jangkep***	enough
Buah-buahan/ **Woh-wohan**	fruits
apokat	avocado
belimbing	starfruit
*biu/**pisang***	banana
durên	durian (famous for its strong smell)
gedang	papaya
juuk Bali	pomelo
juuk semaga	mandarin orange
lêci	lychee
manas	pineapple
manggis	mangosteen
markisa	passion fruit
nangka	jackfruit
nyambu	rambutan
nyambu mentê	cashew nut
*nyuh/**kelapa***	coconut
poh	mango
salak	salak or snakefruit, crispy white fruit with brown scaly skin (nowhere better than in Bali!)
semangka	watermelon

⇨ ⇨ ⇨ ⇨ ⇨ ⇨ ⇨ ⇨ ⇨ ⇨ ⇨ ⇨ ⇨ ⇨   **Market Day**

The oldest members of your party will have the best luck bargaining *di peken wiadin di warung*, in the market or in the stall. Younger Balinese venders may be inclined to demand somewhat higher prices from younger tourists. But they are too shy to do the same with their seniors.

In the Art Shop ⇦ ⇦ ⇦ ⇦ ⇦ ⇦ ⇦ ⇦ ⇦ ⇦ ⇦ ⇦

arca	wooden statue of a god/ goddess
buk*a*/**sekadi**	as
gambar	picture
g*a*gambaran	painting
kayu/**taru**	wood
kulit/**pemulu**	skin, leather
slak*a*	silver
suci/**nirmal*a***	holy, purified
togog	figure, statue, wooden doll
wayang/**ringgit**	shadowplay figure, shadowplay performance
sekadi togog	as a statue (very silent, not speaking anything)

It's not possible to leave Bali without buying a *gagambaran* painting or *togog* sculpture. Surprisingly enough, there's no specific word for "art" in *bas*a* Bali*. You'll find art in the galleries or art shops or, most interestingly, in the house of a *tukang gambar* (master artist). Some artists prefer to speak *bas*a* kasar* or *madi*a*, others *alus*. So the following phrases are given in both versions:

*Gambar enê bagus pesan. Ap*a* isin gambaranê?*

Gambar puniki becik pisan. (Pu)napi daging gambaranê?

This picture is very nice. What's the picture's subject? (*isin*/**daging**=contents or "flesh" of something)

Enê satua unduk Rangda muah Barong.
Puniki katuturan indik Rangda miwah Barong.
The story is about Rangda and Barong

Ada (ke) gambar misin igel-igelan Lêgong?
Wênten (ke) gambar madaging ilên-ilên Lêgong?
Do you have a painting on the Lêgong dance?

Ada di têmbokê baduur-tiang lakar nuunang ento, inggih!
Wênten ring têmbokê baduur—titiang pacang nedunang punika, inggih!
There's (one) on the wall, high up—I will take it down, yes Sir!

Gambar enê aji kuda?
Gambar puniki ajinê aji kuda?
How much does the painting cost?

Gambar enê gaêna becik pisan, ajinê samas tali.
Gambar puniki karyananga becik pisan, ajine samas tali.
This painting is a very nice piece of work; its price is 400 thousand rupiah.

Asking Directions ✧ ✧ ✧ ✧ ✧ ✧ ✧ ✧ ✧ ✧ ✧

dalem	*jero*	inside, deep
dini	*iriki*	here
ditu	*irika*	there
di	*ring*	in
di jaba	*ring jaba*	outside
dija	*ring dija*	where?
kija	*lunga kija*	to where?
ditu	*irika*	there
joh	*doh*	far
jalan/marga	*margi*	way
majalan,	*mamarga,*	1) walk, go
jalan	*marga*	2) carry out
enu	*kari*	still
kema	*merika*	to there
luas	*lunga*	go, come
pesu	*medal*	out
tegeh	*duur*	high
tlaga	*danu*	lake
gunung	*giri*	mountain
tukad	*luah*	river
pasih	*segara*	sea, ocean
titi	*kereteg*	bridge, path

Once I overheard in a Balinese restaurant:

Patakon: **Ring dija** kamar kecil?
Question: Where is the rest room?

Pasaut: Jalan ngauhang—lantas!

Answer: Go to the west—straight on!

Para anak Bali know intuitively which direction is north, and they will always give directions according to the four points of the compass. Asked for the way, they will never tell you to go to the right (*tengawan*/**tengen**) or to the left (*kêbot*/**kiwa**, as in *lima kêbot*, left hand). They will point you east, west, south or north. They will do the same even if they are speaking Indonesian or English.

		north		
		kaja		
		kalêr		
west	*kauh*	+	*kangin*	east
	kulon		**wêtan**	
		kelod		
		kidul		
		south		

The *kasar* directions are the more important to learn. Also note the following:

kaja   inland, toward the mountains (the prosperous direction), meaning north in Southern and Central Bali, south in Bulêlêng (Northern Bali).

kelod   toward the sea (the disastrous direction), meaning south in Southern and Central Bali, north in Bulêlêng.

Asking Directions ⟵⟵⟵⟵⟵ ⟵⟵⟵⟵⟵

The affix *ng– –ang* means "toward," "in the direction of," "–ward":

ngauhang	toward the west, westward
nganginang	toward the east, eastward
ngajanang	toward the north, northward
ngelodang	toward the south, southward

The prefix *d–* means "facing":

dauh	facing west
dangin	facing east
daja	facing north
delod	facing south

majalan nganginang to go eastward

Dija tongos bajunê? Where is the "shirt" place?
Di bale dangin! In the house facing east!

A typical Balinese court will have four buildings—houses or pavilions—each oriented in a different direction of the compass. Hence the *paribasa*, proverb: *Sing nawang kangin-kauh*,
He doesn't know the east from the west. (He doesn't know anything.)

Lunga kija?
Where are you going?

Tiang lakar ka Pura Besakih.
I want to go to Pura Besakih.

Lakar majalan?
Do you want to go by foot?

Inggih*! Ada* **(wênten)** *jalan lurus kema?*
Yes! Is there a path straight to there?

Ada **(wênten)**—*lantas ka dêsa paling paek. Di pem-patanê lantas nganginang.*
There is. Go straight into the nearest village. At the main intersection, go straight toward the east.

Yêning nepukin titi, ditu ngajanang!
When you see a path, (go) to the north from there!

Kari joh?
Is it still far?

Joh pesan!
It is very far!

Remember, "right" and "left" may never be used for directions!

Festivals ⟡⟡⟡⟡⟡⟡⟡⟡⟡⟡ ⟡⟡⟡⟡⟡⟡

Sang Hyang Widi Wasa	God as the ultimate reality
dêwa	god as one of the aspects of **Sang Hyang Widi Wasa**
dêwi	goddess as one of the aspects of **Sang Hyang Widi Wasa**
buta-kala	destroying spirits or demons
kahyangan	abode of the gods, heaven, temple
kahyangan tiga	system of three temples belonging to one *dêsa* (village):
pura puseh	temple for the divine ancestors
pura dêsa	village temple (for the living)
pura dalem	underworld temple (for the dead)
pura	temple
jaba, Jaba	outer court of the temple, outside; member of the rice farmers caste
jaba tengah	middle court of a temple
jeroan	inner court of a temple
jero, Jero	inside; an "insider," member of a higher caste

The Balinese year consists of 210 days. Most temples celebrate their **odalan** (temple festival) once within this 210 day-cycle. (Similarly, the Balinese celebrate their birthday once every 210 days.) However, some **odalan**, as well as other festivals follow another annual cycle—the Hindu-Javanese *saka* or year with 355 days!

Most **odalan** last three days, but can go up to five, seven, nine or even eleven days. For this festival the priests/leaders of the community will invite the *dêwa* and *dêwi* connected with their temple, to come and stay there. The entire community visits the temple to enjoy a big festival together with the *dêwa dêwi*. Each community or family has its own temple. Hence a family **odalan** is celebrated in the family temple, and a village *odalan* will be celebrated by the entire *dêsa* community in one of the three village temples, the **kahyangan tiga**.

abên	**palebon**	cremation
ngabên	**palebon**	celebrate a cremation
dêwasa		auspicious day (for an enterprise)
alihang dêwasa malu		look for an auspicious day first.
nyumunin	**ngawitin**	start
punyan	**wit**	tree, trunk, starting point
paek	**nampek (tampek)**	next
dina/**rahina**		day

Festivals ❖❖❖❖❖❖❖❖❖❖ ❖❖❖❖❖❖

Radite, Raditia	Sunday
Soma	Monday
Anggara	Tuesday
Buda	Wednesday
Wrespati	Thursday
Sukra	Friday
Saniscara	Saturday

To find out *buin pidan?* (when?) and *dija?* (where?) a festival will take place, you may ask the people who are decorating a *pura*, temple. Or, you may ask people sitting around a *warung*. After a little small talk about your name and where you're from, you may ask:

*Ada **odalan** dini di dêsa enê?*
Will there be a temple festival here in this village?

Tusing ada odalan dini, ada ditu, di dêsa Kadêwatan.
There will not be a festival here. There is one over there, in Kadêwatan village.

Di pura encên?
In which temple?

*Di pura dêsa lakar ada **odalan gedê pesan**!*
In the village temple there will be a very big festival!

Buin pidan lakar nyumunin?
When will it start?

Tusing tawang! Melahan takonang di dêsa ento!
I don't know! Better ask in the village over there!

Di warung paek pura desa Kadêwatan:
(In a stall near the temple village Kadêwatan):

Buin pidan **odalan** *di pura desa lakar nyumunin?*
When will the festival in the temple village start?

Odalan *nyumunin* **rahina** *Buda.*
The festival starts on Wednesday.

Kudang dina **odalanê**?
How many days will the festival last?

Limang dina!
Five days!

*Ada anak ngabên/***palebon*** *dini?*
Will there be a man cremated here? (*abên*=cremation
of a *Jaba,* **palebon**=cremation of a ***Triwangsa*)**

Tusing jani, tusing ada dêwasa.
Not now, it is not an auspicious day. (*dêwasa*=
mature, auspicious)

73

Body Language ✧✧✧✧✧✧ ✧✧✧✧✧✧

Go smoothly!

Violent gestures give rise to anxiety. Do not point directly toward someone with the finger. When sitting or lying down, do not point at someone with the feet. Standing akimbo (hands on hips) or crossing your arms over the chest will be perceived as very aggressive behavior. Instead, place your arms behind the back, grasping your left forearm with your right hand.

Better sit down!

For westerners it is polite to stand when greeting somebody. But in Bali—especially during a ceremony such as an *odalan* temple festival—it is best to look for a seat or squat down as soon as possible. It's very offensive when the head of a foreigner towers above the head of an officiating priest. In Balinese tradition, only the priest was allowed to stand; others would have to walk crab-like on the ground.

And please do not climb onto the walls of a *pura* or houseyard! In Bali it is advisable to make yourself as humble, literally as low, as possible.

Watch what you wear!

Proper dress is expected if you want to join a celebration. In the west, no one will enter a church, theater or music hall dressed in a swimsuit. If we see some tourists in Bali doing so, we should inform them that their behavior isn't very proper. To visit a *pura* you are expected to wear a *slempot* (sash: Indonesian *selendang*). When you attend an **odalan** it is your obligation to wear a *sarung* as well. Please follow the local custom!

Learn to smile!

*Kenyem/**kenying***, smiling, is always the best means of good communication. Beware, however, that Balinese smiling is a human complaisance but never, never, never a "come-on" or erotic advance. Balinese may smile if they are embarrassed or anxious or, sometimes, if they are sad or mourning. Smiling can express a very agreeable emotion, but it may express as well the attempt to change a disagreeable feeling into a positive one.

Laugh!

Para anak Bali like to be funny. A proper joke is always welcomed. If you encounter some difficulty or misunderstanding, you may be able to clear the air with a joke. The Balinese like to laugh and they like it if you are laughing too!

Glossary ✧ ✧ ✧ ✧ ✧ ✧ ✧ ✧ ✧ ✧ ✧ ✧ ✧ ✧ ✧

Everyday Balinese

If only one Balinese term appears among the columns, it can be used in the simple as well as in the high language.

Everyday Balinese	High Balinese	English
aa, ya, nggih	*inggih*	yes, sure, right
aa	*patut*	yes, sure, really
abedik	*akedik*	few
pengabênan	*palebon*	cremation
ada	*wênten*	there is/are
adan	*wasta, parab*	name
adat, biasa		custom, *adat*
adêng-adêng	*alon-alon*	slowly
adep	*adol*	sell (to sell)
adep, ngadep	*adol, ngadol*	sell
adi luh	*ari, rai*	sister (younger)
adi muani	*ari*	brother (younger)
aduh	*aduh*	oh!
adung	*patuh*	agreed
ajak, ngajak	*sareng*	(together) with
ajengan	*rayunan*	meal
aji		from (material)
aji	*pangarga*	price

akejep	**ajebos**	at once
aksama	**ampura**	pardon
aluh	**dangan**	easy
alus	**lues**	fine, distinguished
anak	**oka**	man, child
anak jaba	**sudra**	rice farmers, caste
anak luh	**anak istri**	woman
anak muani	**anak lanang**	man (male)
anak tuara	**anak lara**	poor
anê	**sanê**	what, who
anê engkên?	**sanê encên?**	which one, which of them?
pengantênan		bride or groom
anut		fitting, suitable
apa?	**punapi? napi?**	what?
apakrana	**punapi awinan?**	why?
apang	**mangda**	so that
apokat		avocado
arep	**ring arep**	near to, before
asing, asing-asing		whatever, whoever
asri		beautiful (view, ornament)
ati	**pepusuh**	heart

Glossary ✧✧✧✧✧✧✧✧✧✧ ✧✧✧✧✧

awanan	*awinan*	cause (of)
ba (dauh)	*ba (kulon)*	direction to (West)
baan, tekên	*antuk*	from (passive), because of
baang, ngemaang	*icên, ngicên*	give
banjar		autonomous hamlet
banyolan	*baudan*	joke
bapa	*aji*	father
barang		package
bareng-bareng	*sareng-sareng*	together
basa		tongue, language, spices
batik		batik
baya		danger
bê	*ulam*	fish, meat
bê guling		suckling pig (pork)
bêbêk	*pitik*	duck
beli	*raka*	brother (older)
beli, meli	*tumbas, numbas*	buy
belimbing		starfruit
beneh	*patut*	true
betên	*sor*	low, below

bêtutu		prepared meal (poultry)
biasa	**lumrah**	usual
bisa	**sida**	can
biu	**pisang**	banana
bojog	**wenara**	ape
	brahmana	priestly caste
buah		fruit, betel
buin	**malih**	still
buin mani	**bênjang**	tomorrow
buin pidan?	**malih pidan?**	when? (future)
buka	**sekadi, alah**	as
buku	**kitab**	book
bunga	**sekar**	flower
buntut, batis	**cokor**	foot
buta-kala		destroying spirits
caru		offering for the nether world
celep, macelep	**ranjing, nga-ngranjing, ranjing**	enter! come in! to enter
cenik, cerik	**alit**	little
cicing	**asu**	dog
corah	**kaon**	bad
cucu	**putu**	grandchild (girl or boy)

Glossary ⇐⇐⇐⇐⇐⇐⇐⇐ ⇐⇐⇐⇐⇐⇐

dadi	**dados**	become, be able, may
dadong	**nini**	grandmother
dagang, toko		shop
dalang		puppeteer
dalem	**jero**	deep, below, inside
damar	**sundih**	lamp
danê	**ida**	they
danu	**ranu**	lake
demen (tekên)	**seneng (tekên)**	like (something)
	dedari	heavenly nymph
darma		religion
dêsa		village
	dêwa	god
dêwasa		auspicious day
	dêwata	deity
	dêwi	goddess
di	**ring**	in (location), on (time)
di jaba	**ring jaba**	outside
di kenkene		sometimes
di uri, duri	**ring ungkur**	there behind
dibi	**ring dibi**	yesterday
dija?	**ring dija?**	where?
dina	**rahina**	day

dinanê jani	**rahinanê** **mangkin**	today
dingeh, ningeh	**pireng,** **mireng, miarsa**	hear, heard
dingin		cold
dini	**iriki**	here
ditu	**irika**	there
durên		durian
eda	**sampunang**	do not!
encên?	**sanê encên?**	what? which? which one?
enê	**puniki**	this, these, this is
ênggal	**gelis**	quick, prompt
ento	**punika**	that, that is/are
enu	**kari, kantun**	still, remaining
gaêna	**karyananga**	worked out
gambar		picture
	gambelan	gamelan orchestra
gancang, gangsar	**gelis**	quick
gedang		papaya
gedê	**ageng**	big (great)
gagambaran		painting
gelang		bracelet
genep	**jangkep**	enough

Glossary ✧✧✧✧✧✧✧✧✧ ✧✧✧✧✧✧

gênggong		Jew's-harp
goak		crow
godoh		fried banana
	gong	gong
	gria	house (of Brahmana)
gula	**gendis**	sugar
guling		spit roasted
guling cêlêng		suckling pig
gumi	**jagat**	1) world, earth 2) soil, land, territory
gunung	**giri**	mountain
guru		teacher, father
i		the (for persons only)
i raga makejang	**sareng sami**	we
ia	**ipun, ida**	he, she, it
ibanê	**raganê**	by himself, herself, itself
idep	**daging kayun**	purpose
igel-igelan	**ilên-ilên**	dance
indayang		try
inem-ineman	**nginem**	drink
inget	**êling**	wish (to wish)
isi	**daging**	content

jaba	**mijil/jaba**	out, outside
jaba tengah		middle court of a temple
jaen, jaan	**becik**	delicious
jaja	**sesanganan**	rice flour cake
jalan	**marga**	road, way, trip, travel
jani	**mangkin**	now
jegêg	**ayu**	beautiful (nice)
jemak	**ambil**	taken
jengah	**mêrang**	ashamed and angry
jero		house (of *wesia*)
jeroan		inner court of a temple
joh	**doh, adoh**	far
jukut urab	**jejanganan**	mixed vegetable
juuk Bali		pomelo
juuk semaga		mandarin orange
ka	**ring**	to, for
kacang		nuts
kadutan	**keris**	kris,
kaja	**kalêr**	towards the mountains (in Southern Bali: north, in Buleleng: south)

Glossary ✧✧✧✧✧✧✧✧✧ ✧✧✧✧✧✧

kangin	**wêtan**	East direction
karoan	**janten**	sure, certain
kasar		rough, not refined
kasêp	**kasêp**	late
kauh	**kulon**	West direction
	kahyangan	place of the Gods, heaven, temple
kayu	**taru**	wood
kebus	**panes**	hot
kelih	**duur**	grown up, grow up
kelihan	**duuran**	one that is grown up
kelihan banjar		head of a hamlet
kelod	**kidul**	towards the sea (in Southern Bali: south)
kema	**merika**	(to) there
kendel	**rena**	happy
kenê	**asapuniki, saspunika**	so
keneh	**kayun**	thinking, believe
kênkên	**sapunapi**	how?
kenyem	**kenying, kenyir**	smile

ketil	**abot**	difficult
kêto	**kênten**	like this, so
kêweh	**mêweh**	difficult
kija?	**lunga kija?**	where to?
	kiwa	left
klambi	**kuaca**	blouse, jacket
koja, suud, marerên, rêrênang	**usan**	Do not do this any more !, Stop it !
konê	**kocap**	is ordered, is said
kopi	**wêdang kopi**	coffee
krananê (krana)		also, therefore, because (cause)
kruna	**suara**	word
	ksatria	ruler and warrior caste
kuang	**kirang**	less
kuangin	**kirangin**	reduce, less
kuda?		how much? how many?
kulit	**carma**	skin, leather,
kunci		key
kuning	**jenar**	yellow
kuno	**nguni**	old (ancient)
kurenan	**rabi**	wife
kurenan	**swami**	husband, spouse
lakar, bakal	**pacang, jagi, jaga**	shall, will, want, desire

Glossary ✧✧✧✧✧✧✧✧✧ ✧✧✧✧✧✧

lantas	**raris**	straight on
lawar		shredded coconut with spices and meat
lêci		lychee
legu		mosquito
lek, lek ati	**wirang**	ashamed, shy
lelipi	**ula**	snake
lên	**lian**	other, others
lên, bêda	**lian, tios**	different
len-lenan	**lian-lianan**	and other things
liu	**akêh**	much, many
	lontar	palmleaf for writing
losmên		homestay, lodge
luas	**lunga**	go, depart,
luh	**wadon**	female
luih		last
maan (baan)	**polih**	get from, receive from
mabasa (basa)		spicy
mabasa (basa)	**maturin (atur)**	call,
ngomong, ngraos	**ngandika**	speak
maca	**wasen**	read
maca (baca)		read
madan (adan)	**mawasta (wasta)**	to be called

madaar	**ngajeng**	have a meal
mael	**maal**	expensive
magancangin		speed up
mai	**mriki**	please come here
mai ja	**mriki**	come here
majalan (jalan)	**mamarga (marga)**	go, go by foot (way, trip)
kenehang	**makayun**	think (to think)
makejang	**sami, samian**	all
makelo	**sué**	long time
makeneh, makeneh-keneh	**mepikayun**	think, suspect
makurenan		married
makurenan	**marabian**	marry, married
malajah (ajah)		learn
malu	**dumun**	formerly, before
manain	**mecikang**	improve
manas		pineapple
mandus, manjus	**masiram (siram)**	bathe, take a bath
manggis		mangosteen
mara	**wawu**	to come, to arrive
markisa		passion fruit
masambel		containing *sambel*

Glossary ⇦⇦⇦⇦⇦⇦⇦⇦⇦⇦⇦⇦⇦⇦

masatua (satua)	**nutur (tutur)**	tell a story
masaur (saur)		answer (to answer)
masaut (saut)		answer (to answer)
masih	**taler**	also, too, as well
matakon (takon)	**matakên**	ask
matetawahan	**malinggih**	bargaining for
maumah		dwell, stay
mawanan	**mawinan**	also, therefore, because
mayah (bayah)	**naur (taur)**	pay
mbok	**raka**	sister (older)
meh		possible
melah	**becik**	good, beautiful
mêmê	**biyang, ibu**	mother
mêmê bapa	**rerama**	parents
nyêwa (sewa)	**nyêwang**	hire (to hire)
	meru	wooden tower in temple for a deity
	minakadi	extremely, last
minggu	**wuku, minggu**	week
mirib	**menawi**	perhaps
misan	**mingsiki**	cousin
misi (isi)	**madaging (daging)**	containing (contents)

montor		car
muah	**miwah**	and
muani	**lanang**	male
mudah	**murah**	cheap
mula		though, naturally
	naga	dragon, mythological snake
nanging	**sakewanten**	but
nangka		jackfruit
nasak, tasak	**tasak**	ripe
nasi	**ajengan**	boiled rice (meal)
nasi bira		yellow rice
negak (tegak)	**malinggih**	sit (to sit)
negakin		take place, to mount
negera	**negara, jagat**	country, territory
ngaba (aba)	**makta**	bring, carry
ngadanin (adan)	**ngawastanin (wasta)**	to call, to name
ngaê (gaê)	**(ma)karya**	work
ngalih, alih	**ngrereh, rereh**	look for
		open
ngampakang	**ngandika (andika)**	order (to order), say

Glossary ⇦⇦⇦⇦⇦⇦⇦⇦⇦ ⇦⇦⇦⇦⇦⇦

nganggo (anggo)	**nganggê** (anggê)	dress
nganggon (anggon)	**nganggên** (anggên)	take, use
nganti	**ngantosang**	wait
ngawanang	**ngawinang**	cause (to cause)
	ngawitin (wit)	start (tree, origin)
ngelah (gelah)	**maduê (duê)**	have, possess
ngeng		feeling uneasy with
ngerti, resep	**midep**	understand
nyidang	**sida**	can, to be able
ngidih (idih)	**lungsur, nunas (runas)**	beg for
ngisinin	**nagingin**	fill (to fill)
	ngodalin (odal)	celebrate *odalan* (out)
ngomong	**ngraos (raos)**	speak, talk (word, speech)
ngorahin	**majarin**	inform, notify
nguda	**anom**	young
nguda? ngudiang	**punapi awinan**	why?
ngulgul (gulgul)		bother
ningalin (tingal)	**nepukin (tepuk)**	see, look

nomer	**nomer**	number
nongos	**malinggih**	stay
nuju (tuju)		aim toward, agree (aim)
nuju dina	**nuju rahinan**	this day
nulungin (tulung)	**nulungin**	help
nusa	**pulo**	island
nyak	**kayun**	want
nyama	**semeton sanê lanang**	brother
nyama	**semeton sanê istri**	sister
nyama-braya	**semeton**	family
nyambu		waterapple
nyambu mentê		cashew nut
nyambung, nutugan (sambung)	**nglantungan**	keep connection
nyandang	**jangkep**	enough
nyên?	**sira?**	who?
nyinahang (sinahang)		explain, make clear
nyuh	**kelapa**	coconut
nyumunin (jumu)	**ngawitin (wit)**	start
odah	**lingsir**	old (aged)
	odalan	temple festival

Glossary ✧✧✧✧✧✧✧✧✧ ✧✧✧✧✧✧

		origin
orta	**orti**	news, message
paad		flu
pada	**sami**	1) same 2) all
padaang teken	**banding ring**	compared with
padi	**pantun**	rice growing in the field
paek	**nampek, tampek**	near, next
pah,bagi		divided
pamangku		temple priest (usually from *Jaba* caste)
panak, pianak	**oka**	child
pang telu	**ping tiga**	three times
	pangandika	order (the order), word
panganggo	**panganggê,**	clothing
pagelahan	**duê**	property
paon	**perantenan, pawaregan**	kitchen
para		group of persons
paribasa		proverb
pasaut		answer (the answer)
pasih	**segara**	sea
patakon	**patakên**	question

patuh tekên	**pateh ring/ p. sakadi**	equal (=)
	pedanda	brahmana priest
pekak, kak	**kakiang**	grandfather
peken	**pasar**	market
pepes		pin, pinned
pesan	**pisan**	very
pesu	**medal**	out
peteng	**wengi**	dark
peteng	**wengi**	night
pianak luh	**oka istri**	daughter
pianak muani	**oka lanang**	son
pidan?	**ring pidan?**	when? (past)
pijet		flashlight
pipis	**jinah**	money
pocol		loss, bad luck
poh		mango
potrêt		photo
pragat	**puput**	ready, finished
pukul	**dauh, jam**	hour
punyan	**wit**	tree, trunk,
	pura	Hindu temple
	puri	palace, house of *ksatria*
puyung	**tan madaging**	empty
raganê	**jero**	you
	raksasa	demonic giant

Glossary ✧✧✧✧✧✧✧✧✧ ✧✧✧✧✧✧

	raksasi	demonic giantess
	rarisang	please
rerama		uncle, aunt
resep tekên, ngares	*resep ring*	to understand, concept
restoran		restaurant
sabilang	*sanangken*	every
sabun		soap
sai-sai	*sering*	often
sajaba	*sajaba punika*	except
sakêwala	*sakêwanten*	but
salak		salak fruit
sambel		sambal (spicy sidedish)
sampi	*bantêng*	cow
	Sang Hyang Widi Wasa	god as the ultimate reality
sarung	*kamben*	hip-cloth
sastra	*aksara*	letter
saté		satay, small meat pieces on skewers
satua	*katuturan*	story
seger	*kênak*	healthy
sekaa		organization, society
selid sanja	*sepanjang rahina*	all day

semangka	.	water melon
semengan ruput	*semeng*	early morning
sepêda		bike
siap	*ayam*	chicken
sinah		light, clear, distinct
sing, tusing, tuara	*tan, nênten*	no, not
slaka		silver
slempot		sash
soca		jewel
soto babad		tripe soup
suba	*sampun*	already
subak		irrigation cooperative
suci	*nirmala*	holy, purified
sugih	*kaya*	rich
tamiu		guest
tangar	*yatna*	careful
tanggal		date
tawah, nawah		bargain
tawang	*uning*	know (to know)
tegeh	*duur*	high
teka	*rauh*	come (to come), arrive
tekên	*ring*	1) to, against,

Glossary ⟡⟡⟡⟡⟡⟡⟡⟡⟡ ⟡⟡⟡⟡⟡⟡

		for 2) together with 3) of, from (passive) 4) and 5) compared with
telah	*telas*	finished
sedia	*tragia*	ready
tembok		wall
tengah	*madia*	middle
tengatah		yard, courtyard
tengawan	*tengen*	right
tepukin, nepukin	*panggihin manggihin*	see somebody, meet
tetep	*sekayang*	always
tiang	*titiang*	I
tiban	*warsa*	year
timpal	*sawitra*	friend
titi		path, small bridge
tiwas	*miskin*	poor
togog	*arca*	statue
tondên, kondên	*durung*	not yet
tongos	*linggih*	place, location
topêng	*tapel*	mask, mask performance
tresna	*asih*	love
	triwangsa	three noble classes

tuah	**wantah**	only
tuak	**sajeng**	palm wine
tukad		river
tukang		master, specialist
tukang gambar	**asli**	painter
tulén	**nulungin**	original
tuni	**i ketuni**	just
tusing, sing, tuara	**tan, nênten**	no, not
tutur	**piteket**	advice
tuturan	**ceritera**	story
tuuh	**yusa**	age
tuunang	**tedunang**	take down
ua	**bibi**	aunt
ua, wa	**paman**	uncle
uli	**saking**	from
uli dija?	**saking napi**	where from?
uma	**carik**	paddyfield,
umah		house (of a jaba)
umpama	**tetiladan**	example
unduk	**indik**	for, about
duri	**ungkur**	behind
urutan celeng		pork sausages
warna	**warni**	color
warung		booth, foodstall
wayang	**ringgit**	shadowplay

Glossary ✧✧✧✧✧✧✧✧✧✧✧✧✧✧✧

		figure
wayang kulit		shadow play
	wêsia	officials caste
dagang	**pengadol, saudagar**	merchants
wiadin	**utawai**	or
	widiadari, dedari	heavenly nymph
wikan	**wicaksana**	clever with
yeh	**toya**	water
	tirta	holy water
yên, yan	**yêning**	if

High Balinese

High Balinese	Everyday Balinese	English
abot	*ketil*	difficult
	adat, biasa	custom, *adat*
adokang, ngadokang	*adep, ngadep*	meet (to meet face to face)
adol	*adep*	sell (to sell)
ageng	*gedê*	big (great)
ajebos	*akejep*	at once
ajengan	*nasi*	boiled rice (meal)
aji	*bapa*	father
akedik	*abedik*	few
akêh	*liu*	much, many
aksara	*sastra*	letter
alit	*cenik, cerik*	little
alon-alon	*adêng-adêng*	slow-slow, slowly
ambil	*jemak*	taken
ampura	*aksama*	pardon
anak istri	*anak luh*	woman
anak lanang	*anak muani*	man (male)
anom	*nguda*	young
antuk	*baan, tekên*	from (pass.), because of

Glossary ✧✧✧✧✧✧✧✧✧✧ ✧✧✧✧✧✧

antun	nyambung (sambung)	keep connection
	anut	fitting, suitable
arca	togog	statue
ari	adi muani	brother (younger)
ari, rai	adi luh	sister (younger)
asapuniki, sapunika	kênê	so
asih	tresna	love
asu	cicing	dog
awinan	awanan	cause (of)
ayam	siap	chicken
ayu	jegêg	beautiful (nice)
ba (kulon)	ba (dauh)	direction to (West)
banding ring	padaang tekên	compared with
	banjar	autonomous hamlet
bantêng	sampi	cow
baudan	banyolan	joke
becik	melah	good, beautiful
bênjang	buin mani	tomorrow
bibi	ua	aunt
biyang, ibu	mêmê	mother
brahmana		priestly caste
carik	uma	paddyfield

carma	kulit	skin, leather
ceritera	tuturan	story
cokor	buntut, batis	foot
dados	dadi	become, be able, may
daging	isi	content
daging kayun	idep	purpose
dalang	dalang	puppeteer
dangan	aluh	easy
darma	darma	religion
dêwa		god
dêwata		deity
dêwi		goddess
doh, adoh	joh	far
duê	pagelahan	property
dumun	malu	formerly, before
durung	tondên, kondên	not yet
duur	kelih	grown up, grow up
duur	tegeh	high
duuran	kelihan	one, that is grown up
êling	inget	wish (to wish)
	makeneh, makeneh-keneh	think, suspect
	nyinahang (sinahang)	explain, make clear

Glossary ✧✧✧✧✧✧✧✧✧✧✧✧✧✧✧

gambelan		gamelan orchestra
gelis	*ênggal*	quick, prompt
gelis	*gancang, gangsar*	quick
gendis	*gula*	sugar
gong		gong
gria		house (of Brahmana)
i ketuni	*tuni*	just
icên, ngicên	*baang, ngemaang*	give
ida	*danê*	they
ilên-ilên	*igel-igelan*	dance
indik	*unduk*	for, about
nampek	*paek*	near to, before
inggih	*aa, saja, nggih*	yes, sure, right
ipun, ida	*ia*	he, she, it
irika	*ditu*	there
iriki	*dini*	here
jagat	*gumi*	1) world, earth 2) soil, land, territory
jangkep	*genep*	enough
jangkep	*nyandang*	enough
janten	*karoan*	sure, certain
jajanganan	*jukut urab*	mixed vegetable

jenar	*kuning*	yellow
jero	*dalem*	deep, below, inside
jero	*jero*	house (of *wesia*)
jero	*raganê*	you
jeroan	*jeroan*	inner court of a temple
jinah	*pipis*	money
kakiang	*pekak, kak*	grandfather
kaler	*kaja*	towards the mountains (in Southern Bali: north, in Buleleng: south)
kamben	*sarung*	hip-cloth
kari, kantun	*enu*	still, remaining
karyananga	*gaêna*	worked out
katuturan	*satua*	story
kaya	*sugih*	rich
kahyangan		place of the Gods, heaven, temple
pepusuh	*ati*	heart
kayun	*keneh*	thinking, believe
kayun	*nyak*	want
	kelihan banjar	head of a hamlet
kênak	*seger*	healthy

Glossary ✧ ✧ ✧ ✧ ✧ ✧ ✧ ✧ ✧ ✧ ✧ ✧ ✧ ✧ ✧

kênten	*kêto*	like this, so
kenying	*kenyem*	smile
keris	*kadutan*	kris, special dagger
kidul	*kelod*	towards the sea (in Southern Bali: south)
kirang	*kuang*	less
kirangin	*kuangin*	reduce, less
kitab	*buku*	book
kiwa		left
klapa	*nyuh coconut*	coconut
kocap	*konê*	is ordered, is said
ksatria		ruler and warrior caste
kuaca	*klambi*	blouse, jacket
kulon	*kauh*	West direction
lanang	*muani*	male
lara	*tiwas*	poor
lian	*lên*	other, others
lian, tios	*lên, bêda*	different
lian-lianan	*lên-lênan*	and other things
linggih	*tongos*	place, location
lingsir	*odah*	old (aged)
luwes	*alus*	fine, distinguished

lumrah	biasa	usual
lunga	luas	go, depart
lunga kija?	kija?	where to?
lungsur, nunas (tunas)	ngidih (idih)	beg for
madaging (daging)	misi (isi)	containing (content)
madia	tengah	middle
maduê (duê)	ngelah (gelah)	have, possess
majarin	ngorahin	inform, notify
makarya (karya)	ngaê (gaê)	work
makayun		think (to think)
makta	ngaba (aba)	bring, carry
malih	buin	still
malih pidan?	buin pidan?	when? (future)
malinggih	negak (tegak)	sit (to sit)
malinggih	nongos	stay
mamarga (marga)	majalan (jalan)	go, go by foot (way, trip)
mana	encên?	what? which? which one?
mangkin	jani	now
marabian	makurenan	marry, married
marga	jalan	road, way, trip, travel
masiram	mandus,	bathe, take a

Glossary ✧✧✧✧✧✧✧✧✧ ✧✧✧✧✧✧

(siram)	*manjus*	bath
matakên	*matakon (takon)*	ask
maturin (atur)	*mabasa (basa)*	call, speak
mawasta (wasta)	*madan (adan)*	to be called
mawinan	*mawanan*	also, therefore, because
mecikang	*manain*	improve
medal	*pesu*	out
menawi	*mirib*	perhaps
mêrang	*jengah*	ashamed and angry
merika	*kema*	(to) there
meru		wooden tower in temple for a deity
mêweh	*kêweh*	difficult
midep	*ngerti, respe*	understand
mijil/jaba	*jaba*	out, outside
minakadi		extremely, last
mingsiki	*misan*	cousin
miskin	*tiwas*	poor
miwah	*muah*	and
mriki	*mai*	please come here
mriki	*mai ja*	come here

murah	*mudah*	cheap
naga		dragon, mythological snake
nagingin	*ngisinin*	fill (to fill)
nampek, tampek	*paek*	near, next
naur (taur)	*mayah (bayah)*	pay
nepukin (tepuk)	*ningalin (tingal)*	see, look
ngajengan	*inem-ineman*	drink
ngandika (andika)		order (to order), say
nganggê (anggê)	*nganggo (anggo)*	dress, to
nganggên (anggên)	*nganggon (anggon)*	take, use
ngantosang	*ngantiang*	wait
ngawastanin (wasta)	*ngadanin (adan)*	to call, to name
ngawinang	*ngawanang*	cause (to cause)
ngawitin (wit)		start (tree, origin)
ngawitin (wit)	*nyumunin (jumu)*	start
ngodalin (odal)		celebrate *odalan* (out)
ngraos (raos)	*ngomong*	speak, talk

Glossary ✧ ✧ ✧ ✧ ✧ ✧ ✧ ✧ ✧ ✧ ✧ ✧ ✧ ✧ ✧

		(word, speech)
ngrereh, rereh	*ngalih, alih*	look for
nguni	*kuno*	old (ancient)
nini	*dadong*	grandmother
nirmala	*suci*	holy, purified
nutur (tutur)	*masatua (satua)*	tell a story
odalan		temple festival
oka	*panak, pianak*	child
oka istri	*pianak luh*	daughter
		origin
orti	*orta*	news, message
pacang, jagi, jaga	*lakar, bakal*	shall, will, want, desire
palebon	*pengabênan*	cremation
paman	*ua, wa*	uncle
panes	*kebus*	hot
ping tiga	*pang telu*	three times
pangaji	*aji*	price
pangandika		order (the order), word
panganggê	*panganggo*	clothing
panggihin	*tepukin, nepukin*	see somebody, meet
pantun	*padi*	rice growing in the field
pasar	*peken*	market

patakên	*patakon*	question
pateh ring/ p. sakadi	*patuh tekên*	equal (=)
patut	*aa*	yes, sure, really
patut	*beneh*	true
pedanda		brahmana priest
	pijet	flashlight
pireng, mireng	*dingeh, ningeh*	hear, heard
pisan	*pesan*	very
pisang	*biu*	banana
pitik	*bêbêk*	duck
polih	*maan (baan)*	get from, receive from
	portrêt	photo
perantenan, pawaregan	*paon*	kitchen
punapi awinan	*nguda? ngudiang*	why?
punapi? napi?	*apa?*	what?
punika	*ento*	that, that is/are
puniki	*enê*	this, these, this is
puput	*pragat*	ready, finished
pura		Hindu temple
puri		palace, house of Ksatria

Glossary ✧✧✧✧✧✧✧✧✧ ✧✧✧✧✧✧

putra	*pianak muani*	son
putu	*cucu*	grandchild (girl or boy)
rabi	*kurenan*	wife
raganê	*ibanê*	by himself, herself, itself
rahina	*dina*	day
rahinanê mangkin	*dinanê jani*	today
raka	*beli*	brother (older)
raka	*mbok*	sister (older)
raksasa		demonic giant
raksasi		demonic giantess
ranjing nga-ranjingang	*celep nyelepang*	enter! come in! to enter
raris	*lantas*	straight on
rarisang		please
rauh	*teka*	come (to come) arrive
rayunan	*ajengan*	meal
rena	*kendel*	happy
rerama	*mêmê bapa rerama*	parents uncle, aunt
resep ring	*resep tekên, ngares*	understand, concept
ring	*di*	in (location), on (time)

ring	*ka*	to, for
ring	*tekên*	1) to, against, for 2) together with 3) of, from (pass) 4) and 5) compared with
ring dija?	*dija?*	where?
ring jaba	*di jaba*	outside
ring pidan?	*pidan?*	when? (past)
ring ungkur	*di uri, duri*	there behind
ringgit	*wayang*	shadowplay figure
sajaba punika	*sajaba*	except
sajeng	*tuak*	palm wine
sakadi, alah	*buka*	as
sakewanten	*nanging*	but
sakêwanten	*sakêwala*	but
saking	*uli*	from
saking dija	*uli dija?*	where from?
sami	*pada*	1) same 2) all
sami, samian	*makejang*	all
sampun	*suba*	already
sampunang	*eda*	do not!
sanangken	*sabilang*	every
sanê	*anê*	what, who

Glossary ✧✧✧✧✧✧✧✧✧ ✧✧✧✧✧✧

sanê encên?	*anê engkên?*	which one? which of them?
Sang Hyang Widi Wasa		god as the ultimate reality
sapunapi	*kênkên*	how?
sareng	*ajak, ngajak*	(together) with
sareng sami	*i raga makejang*	we
sareng-sareng	*bareng-bareng*	together
sawitra	*timpal*	friend
segara	*pasih*	sea
sekar	*bunga*	flower
sekayang	*tetep*	always
pasêmetonan	*pakurenan*	family
semeton	*nyama*	brother
semeton	*nyama-braya*	family
semeton sanê istri	*nyama*	sister
seneng (tekên)	*demen (tekên)*	like (something)
sepanjang rahina	*selid sanja*	all day
sering	*sai-sai*	often
sasanganan	*jaja*	rice flour cake
sida	*bisa*	can
sida	*ngidang*	can, to be able
sira?	*nyên?*	who?
sor	*betên*	low, below
suara	*kruna*	word

sudra	*anak jaba*	rice farmers caste
sué	*makelo*	long time
sundih	*damar*	lamp
suami	*kurenan*	husband, spouse
taler	*masih*	also, too, as well
tan madaging	*puyung*	empty
tan, nênten	*sing, tusing, tuara*	no, not
tan, nênten	*tusing, sing, tuara*	no, not
tapel	*topêng*	mask, mask performance
taru	*kayu*	wood
telas	*telah*	finished
telas	*telah*	ready
tengen	*tengawan*	right
tetiladan	*umpama*	example
tedunang	*tuunang*	take down
titiang	*tiang*	I
toya	*yêh*	water
tirta		holy water
triwangsa		three noble classes
tumbas, numbas	*beli, meli*	buy
ula	*lelipi*	snake

Glossary ⇦ ⇦ ⇦ ⇦ ⇦ ⇦ ⇦ ⇦ ⇦ ⇦ ⇦ ⇦ ⇦ ⇦ ⇦

ulam	*bê*	fish, meat
punapi awinan	*apakrana*	why?
punapi? napi?	*apa?*	what?
ungkur	*uri*	behind
uning	*tawang*	know (to know)
utawai	*wiadin*	or
wadon	*luh*	female
wantah	*tuah*	only
warni	*warna*	color
wacên	*maca*	read
wasta, nama	*adan*	name
wawu	*mara*	to come, to arrive
wayang kulit	*wayang kulit*	shadow play
wêdang kopi	*kopi*	coffee
wenara	*bojog*	ape
wengên	*peteng*	dark
wengi	*peteng*	night
wênten	*ada*	there is/are
pangadol, saudagar	*dagang*	merchants, officials caste
wêtan	*kangin*	East direction
wicaksana	*wikan*	clever
widiadari, dedari		heavenly nymph

wit	*punyan*	tree, trunk, origin
woh	*buah*	fruit, betel
yatna	*tangar*	careful
yêning	*yên, yan*	if
yusa	*tuuh*	age

Glossary ⬿⬿⬿⬿⬿⬿⬿⬿⬿ ⬿⬿⬿⬿⬿⬿⬿

English

English	Everyday Balinese	High Balinese
advice	*tutur*	*piteket*
against, to	*tekên*	*ring*
age	*tuuh*	*yusa*
agreed	*adung*	
aim toward	*nuju (tuju)*	
agree (aim)		
all	*pada, makejang*	*sami, samian*
all day	*selid sanja*	*sepanjang rahina*
already	*suba*	*sampun*
also, therefore, because (cause)	*mawanan krananê (krana)*	*mawinan*
also, therefore, because	*mawanan*	*mawinan*
also, too, as well	*masih*	*taler*
always	*tetep*	*sekayang*
and	*muah, tekên*	*miwah, ring*
and other things	*lên-lênan*	*lian-lianan*
answer (the	*pasaut*	

answer)		
answer	*masaur (saur)*	
(to answer)	*masaut (saut)*	
ape	*bojog*	***wenara***
as	*buka*	***sakadi, alah***
ashamed		
and angry	*jengah*	***mêrang***
ashamed, shy	*lek, lek ati*	
ask	*matakon*	***matakên***
	(takon)	
at once	*akejep*	***ajebos***
aunt	*ua*	***bibi***
auspicious day	*dêwasa*	
autonomous	*banjar*	
hamlet		
avocado	*apokat*	
bad	*corah*	***kaon***
banana	*biu*	***pisang***
bargain	*tawah, nawah*	
bargaining for	*matetawahan*	
bathe,	*mandus,*	***masiram***
take a bath	*manjus*	***(siram)***
batik	*batik*	
beautiful	*jegêg*	***ayu***
(nice)		
beautiful	*asri*	
(view, ornament)		

Glossary ✧✧✧✧✧✧✧✧✧ ✧✧✧✧✧

become, be able, may	*dadi*	**dados**
beg for	*ngidih (idih)*	**lungsur, nunas (tunas)**
behind	*uri*	**ungkur**
big (great)	*gedê*	**ageng**
bike	*sepêda*	
blouse, jacket	*klambi*	**kuaca**
boiled rice (meal)	*nasi*	**ajengan**
book	*buku*	**kitab**
booth, foodstall	*warung*	
bother	*ngulgul (gulgul)*	
bracelet	*gelang*	
brahmana priest		**pedanda**
bride	*antên*	
bring, carry	*ngaba (aba)*	**makta**
brother	*nyama*	**semeton**
brother (older)	*beli*	**raka**
brother (younger)	*adi muani*	**ari**
but	*nanging sakêwala*	**sakêwanten**
buy	*beli, meli*	**tumbas, numbas**
by himself,	*ibanê*	**raganê**

herself, itself		
call, speak	*mabasa (basa)*	***maturin (atur)***
can	*bisa*	***sida***
can, to be able	*nyidang*	***sida***
car	*montor*	
careful	*tangar*	***yatna***
cashew nut	*nyambu mentê*	
cause (of)	*awanan*	***awinan***
cause (to cause)	*ngawanang*	***ngawinang***
cause, because	*krana*	
celebrate *odalan* (out)		***ngodalin (odal)***
cheap	*mudah*	***murah***
chicken	*siap*	***ayam***
child	*panak, pianak*	***oka***
clever	*wikan*	***wicaksana***
clothing	*panganggo*	***panganggê***
coconut	*nyuh coconut*	***kelapa***
coffee,	*kopi*	***wêdang kopi***
cold	*dingin*	
color	*warna*	***warni***
come (to come), arrive	*teka*	***rauh***
come here	*mai ja*	***mriki***
compared with	*padaang tekên*	***banding ring***

Glossary ⟻ ⟻ ⟻ ⟻ ⟻ ⟻ ⟻ ⟻ ⟻ ⟻ ⟻ ⟻ ⟻ ⟻

compared with	tekên	**ring**
containing (content)	misi (isi)	**madaging (daging)**
containing sambel	masambel	
content	isi	**daging**
country, territory	negara	
cousin	misan	**mingsiki**
cow	sampi	**bantêng**
cremation	pengabênan	**palebon**
crow	goak	
custom, adat	adat, biasa	
dance	igel-igelan	**ilên-ilên**
danger	baya	
dark	peteng	**wengi**
date	tanggal	
daughter	pianak luh	**oka istri**
day	dina	**rahina**
deep, below, inside	dalem	**jero**
deity		**dêwata**
delicious	jaen, jaan	
demonic giant		**raksasa**
demonic giantess		**raksasi**
destroying spirits	buta-kala	

different	*len, bêda*	**lian, tios**
difficult	*ketil*	**abot**
difficult	*kêweh*	**mêweh**
direction to (West)	*ba (dauh)*	**ba (kulon)**
divided	*pah*	
do not!	*eda*	**sampunang**
dog	*cicing*	**asu**
dragon, mythological snake		**naga**
dress	*nganggo (anggo)*	**nganggê (anggê)**
drink	*inem-ineman*	**ngajengan**
duck	*bêbêk*	**pitik**
durian	*durên*	
dwell, stay	*maumah*	
early morning	*semengan ruput*	**semeng**
earth, world	*gumi*	**jagat**
East direction	*kangin*	**wêtan**
easy	*aluh*	**dangan**
empty	*puyung*	**tan madaging**
enough	*genep*	**jangkep**
enough	*nyandang*	**jangkep**
enter! come in!	*celep*	**ranjing**
to enter	*nyelepang*	**ngaranjingang**
equal (=)	*patuh teken*	**pateh ring/ p. sakadi**

Glossary ⟡⟡⟡⟡⟡⟡⟡⟡⟡ ⟡⟡⟡⟡⟡⟡

every	*sabilang*	***sanangken***
example	*umpama*	***tetiladan***
except	*sajaba*	***sajaba punika***
expensive	*mael*	
explain, make clear	*nyinahang (sinahang)*	
extremely, last		***minakadi***
family	*kuren nyama-braya*	***semeton***
far	*joh*	***doh, adoh***
father	*bapa*	***aji***
feeling uneasy with	*ngeng*	
female	*luh*	***wadon***
few	*abedik*	***akedik***
fill (to fill)	*ngisinin*	***nagingin***
fine, distinguished	*alus*	***luwes***
finished	*telah*	***telas***
first, formerly	*anê paling malu*	***sanê pinih riin***
fish, meat	*bê*	***ulam***
fitting, suitable	*anut*	
flashlight	*pijet*	
flower	*bunga*	***sekar***
flu	*paad*	
foot	*buntut, batis*	***cokor***

for, about	*unduk*	*indik*
formerly, before	*malu*	*dumun*
fried banana	*godoh*	
friend	*timpal*	*sawitra*
from (local)	*uli*	*saking*
from (Material)	*aji*	
from (pass.) because of	*baan, tekên*	*antuk*
fruit, betel,	*buah*	
gamelan orchestra		*gambelan*
get from, receive from	*maan (baan)*	*polih*
give	*baang, ngemaang*	*icên, ngicên*
go, depart	*luas*	*lunga*
go, go by foot (way, trip)	*majalan (jalan)*	*mamarga (marga)*
god		*dêwa*
god as the ultimate reality		*Sang Hyang Widi Wasa*
goddess		*dêwi*
gong		*gong*
good, beautiful	*melah*	*becik*
grandchild (girl or boy)	*cucu*	*putu*

Glossary ⟨⟨⟨⟨⟨⟨⟨⟨⟨ ⟨⟨⟨⟨⟨⟨

grandfather	*pekak, kak*	**kakiang**
grandmother	*dadong*	**nini**
groom	*antên*	
group of persons	*para*	
grown up, grow up,	*kelih*	**duur**
one that is grown up	*kelihan*	**duuran**
guest	*tamiu*	
happy	*kendel*	**rena**
have, possess	*ngelah (gelah)*	**maduê (duê)**
he, she, it	*ia*	**ipun, ida**
head of a hamlet	*kelihan banjar*	
healthy	*seger*	**kênak**
hear, heard	*dingeh, ningeh*	**pireng, mireng**
heart	*ati*	**pepusuh**
heavenly nymph		**widiadari, dedari**
help	*nulungin (tulung)*	
here	*dini*	**iriki**
high	*tegeh*	**duur**
Hindu temple		**pura**
hip-cloth	*sarung*	**kamben**
hire (to hire)	*menyêwa (sêwa)*	
holy, purified	*suci*	**nirmala**

homestay, lodge	*losmên*	
hot	*kebus*	*panes*
hour	*pukul*	
house (of a Jaba)	*umah*	
house (of Brahmana)		*gria*
house (of Ksatria)		*puri*
house (of Wesia)	*jero*	
how	*buka*	
how?	*kênkên*	*sapunapi*
how much? how many?	*kuda?*	
husband, spouse	*somah, muani kurenan*	*suami*
I, me	*tiang*	*titiang*
if	*yên, yan*	*yêning*
improve	*manain*	*mecikang*
in, (loc.), on (time)	*di*	*ring*
inform, notify	*ngorahin*	*majarin*
inner court of a temple	*jeroan*	
irrigation cooperative	*subak*	
is ordered, is said	*konê*	*kocap*

Glossary ✧✧✧✧✧✧✧✧✧✧✧✧✧✧✧

island	nusa	
jackfruit	nangka	
Jew's harp	gênggong	
jewel	soca	
joke	banyolan	**baudan**
just	tuni	**i ketuni**
keep connection	nyambung (sambung)	**antun**
key	kunci	
kitchen	paon	**perantenan, pawaregan**
know (to know)	tawang	**uning**
kris, special dagger	kadutan	**keris**
lake	danu	
lamp	damar	**sundih**
last	panyuud	**pamuput pinih ungkur**
late	kasêp	
learn	malajah (ajah)	
left		**kiwa**
less	kuang	**kirang**
letter	sastra	**aksara**
light, clear, distinct	sinah	
like (something)	demen (tekên)	**seneng (tekên)**

like this, so	*kêto*	***kênten***
little	*cenik, cerik*	***alit***
long time	*makelo*	***sué***
look for	*ngalih, alih*	***ngrereh, rereh***
loss, bad luck	*pocol*	
love	*tresna*	***asih***
low, below	*betên*	***sor***
lychee	*lêci*	
male	*muani*	***lanang***
man (male)	*anak muani*	***anak lanang***
man, child	*anak*	
mandarin orange	*juuk semaga*	
mango	*poh*	
mangosteen	*manggis*	
market	*peken*	***pasar***
marry, married	*makurenan*	***marabian***
married	*makurenan*	
mask, mask performance	*topêng*	***tapel***
master, specialist	*tukang*	
meal	*ajengan*	***rayunan***
merchants,	*dagang*	***pangadol saudagar***
officials caste		***wêsia***
middle	*tengah*	***madia***

Glossary ✦✦✦✦✦✦✦✦✦ ✦✦✦✦✦✦

middle court of a temple	*jaba tengah*	
mixed vegetable	*jukut urab*	**jajanganan**
money	*pipis*	**jinah**
mosquito	*legu*	
mother	*mêmê*	**biyang, ibu**
mountain	*gunung*	**giri**
much, many	*liu*	**akêh**
name	*adan*	**wasta, nama**
near to, before	*arep*	**ring arep**
near, next	*paek*	**nampek, tampek**
news, message	*orta*	**orti**
night	*peteng*	**wengi**
no, not	*sing, tusing, tuara*	**tan, nênten**
no, not	*tusing, sing, tuara*	**tan, nênten**
not yet	*tondên, kondên*	**durung**
now	*jani*	**mangkin**
number	*nomer*	
nuts	*kacang*	
of, from (passive)	*tekên*	**ring**
offering for the nether	*caru*	

128

world		
often	*sai-sai*	**sering**
oh!	*aduh*	
old (aged)	*odah*	**lingsir**
old (ancient)	*kuno*	**nguni**
only	*tuah*	**wantah**
open	*ngampakang*	
or	*wiadin*	**utawai**
order (the order), word		**pangandika**
order (to order), say		**ngandika (andika)**
organization, society, origin	*sekaa*	
original	*tulén, mula, jati*	**asli**
other, others	*lên*	**lian**
out	*pesu*	**medal**
out, outside	*jaba*	**mijil, jaba**
outside	*di jaba*	**ring jaba**
package	*barang*	
paddyfield	*uma*	**carik**
painter	*tukang gambar*	
painting	*gagambaran*	
picture		
palace, house of Ksatria		**puri**
palm wine	*tuak*	**sajeng**

Glossary ✧✧✧✧✧✧✧✧✧ ✧✧✧✧✧✧

palmleaf for writing		*lontar*
papaya	*gedang*	
pardon	*aksama*	*ampura*
parents	*mêmê bapa*	*rerama*
passion fruit	*markisa*	
path, small bridge	*titi*	
pay	*mayah (bayah)*	*nauer (taur)*
perhaps	*mirib*	*menawi*
photo	*portrêt*	
picture	*gambar*	
pin, pinned	*pepes*	
pineapple	*manas*	
place of the heaven, temple		*kahyangan*
place, location	*tongos*	*linggih*
please		*rarisang*
please come, here	*mai*	*mriki*
pomelo	*juuk Bali*	
poor	*tiwas, lacur*	*lara*
poor	*tiwas*	*miskin*
poor	*anak tuara*	
pork sausages	*urutan celeng*	
possible	*mêh*	
prepared meal	*bêtutu*	

(poultry)

English		
price	*aji*	**pangaji**
priestly caste		**brahmana**
property	*pagelahan*	**duê**
proverb	*paribasa*	
puppeteer	*dalang*	
purpose	*idep*	**daging kayun**
question	*patakon*	**patakên**
quick	*gancang,* *gangsar*	**gelis**
quick, prompt	*ênggal*	**gelis**
read	*maca*	**wasen**
read	*maca (baca)*	
ready	*sedia*	**tragia**
ready, finished	*pragat*	**puput**
reduce, less	*kuangin*	**kirangin**
religion	*darma*	
restaurant	*restoran*	
rice farmers caste	*anak jaba*	**sudra**
rice flour cake	*jaja*	**sasanganan**
rice growing in the field	*padi*	**pantun**
rich	*sugih*	**kaya**
right	*tengawan*	**tengen**
ripe	*nasak, tasak*	
river	*tukad*	

Glossary ✧✧✧✧✧✧✧✧✧ ✧✧✧✧✧✧

road, way, trip, travel	*jalan*	**marga**
rough, not refined	*kasar*	
ruler and warrior caste		**ksatria**
salak fruit	*salak*	
sambal (spicy sidedish)	*sambel*	
same	*pada*	**sami**
sash	*slempot*	
satay, small meat pieces on skewers	*satê*	
sea	*pasih*	**segara**
see sombody, meet	*tepukin, nepukin*	**panggihin manggihin**
see, look	*ningalin (tingal)*	**nepukin (tepuk)**
sell	*adep, ngadep*	**ngadol, adol**
shadow play	*wayang kulit*	
shadowplay figure	*wayang*	**ringgit**
shall, will, want, desire	*lakar, bakal*	**pacang, jagi, jaga**
shop	*dagang, toko*	
shredded	*lawar*	

English		
coconut with spices and meat		
silver	*slaka*	
sister	*nyama luh*	**semeton sanê istri**
sister (older)	*mbok*	**raka**
sister (younger)	*adi luh*	**ari/rai**
sit (to sit)	*negak (tegak)*	**malinggih**
skin, leather	*kulit*	**carma**
slowly,	*adêng-adêng*	**alon-alon**
smile	*kenyem*	**kenying**
snake	*lelipi*	**ula**
so	*kenê*	**asapuniki, sapunika**
so that	*apang*	**mangda**
soap	*sabun*	
soil, land	*gumi*	**jagat**
sometimes	*di kênkênê*	
son	*pianak muani*	**putra**
speak, talk (word, speech)	*ngomong*	**ngraos (raos)**
speed up	*magancangin*	
spicy	*mabasa (basa)*	
spit roasted	*guling*	
starfruit	*belimbing*	
start	*nyumunin (jumu)*	**ngawitin (wit)**

Glossary ⟵⟡⟡⟡⟡⟡⟡⟡⟡ ⟡⟡⟡⟡⟡⟡

start (tree, origin)		**ngawitin (wit)**
statue	togog	**arca**
stay	nongos	**malinggih**
still	buin	**malih**
still, remaining	enu	**kari, kantun**
story	satua	**katuturan**
story	tuturan	**ceritera**
straight on	lantas	**raris**
suckling pig (pork)	be guling	
suckling pig	guling celeng	
sugar	gula	**gendis**
sure, certain	karoan	**janten**
take down	tuunang	**tedunang**
take place, to mount	negakin	
take, use	nganggon (anggon)	**nganggên (anggên)**
taken	jemak	**ambil**
teacher, father	guru	
tell a story	masatua (satua)	**nutur (tutur)**
temple festival		**odalan**
temple priest (usually from *Jaba* caste)	pamangku	
territory	gumi	**jagat**

134

that, that is/ are	*ento*	**punika**
the (for persons only)	*i*	
there	*ditu*	**irika**
there behind	*di uri, duri*	**ring ungkur**
there is/ are	*ada*	**wenten**
there, to there	*kema*	**merika**
they	*danê*	**ida**
think (to think)	**makayun**	
think, suspect	*makeneh, makeneh-keneh*	
thinking, believe	*keneh*	**kayun**
this, these, this is	*enê*	**puniki**
this day	*nuju dina*	**nuju rahinan**
though, naturally	*mula*	
three noble classes		**triwangsa**
three times	*pang telu*	**ping tiga**
to be called	*madan (adan)*	**mawasta (wasta)**
to call, to name	*ngadanin (adan)*	**ngawastanin (wasta)**
to come,	*mara*	**wawu**

Glossary ⇦⇦⇦⇦⇦⇦⇦⇦⇦⇦⇦⇦⇦⇦

to arrive to there	*kema*	**merika**
to, against	*tekên*	**ring**
to, for	*ka*	**ring**
today	*dinanê jani*	**rahinanê mangkin**
together	*bareng-bareng*	**sareng-sareng**
together with	*ajak, ngajak*	**sareng**
together with	*tekên*	**ring**
tomorrow	*buin mani*	**bênjang**
tongue, language, spices	*basa*	
towards the mountains (in Southern Bali: north, in Buleleng: south)	*kaja*	**kalêr**
towards the sea	*kelod*	**kidul**
tree, trunk	*punyan*	**wit**
tripe soup	*soto babad*	
true	*beneh*	**patut**
try	*indayang*	
uncle	*ua, wa*	**paman**
uncle, aunt	*rerama*	
understand	*ngerti, respe*	**midep**
understand, concept	*resep tekên, ngares*	**resep ring**

usual	*biasa*	**lumrah**
very	*pesan*	**pisan**
village	*dêsa*	
wait	*nganti*	**ngantosang**
wall	*tembok*	
want	*nyak*	**kayun**
water,	*yêh*	**toya**
holy water		**tirta**
water melon	*semangka*	
waterapple	*nyambu*	
we	*i raga*	
	makejang	**sareng sami**
week	*minggu*	
West direction	*kauh*	**kulon**
what, who	*anê*	**sanê**
what?	*apa?*	**punapi? napi?**
what? which?	*encên?*	**mana**
which one?		
whatever,	*asing, asing-*	
whoever	*asing*	
when? (future)	*buin pidan?*	**malih pidan?**
when? (past)	*pidan?*	**ring pidan?**
where from?	*uli dija?*	**saking dija**
where to?	*kija?*	**lunga kija?**
where?	*dija?*	**ring dija?**
which one?	*anê engkên?*	**sanê encên?**
which of them?		

Glossary ✦✦✦✦✦✦✦✦✦✦✦✦✦✦

who?	nyên?	*sira?*
why?	apakrana nguda? ngudiang	*punapi awinan*
wife	kurenan	*rabi*
wish (to wish)	inget	*êling*
with, together with	ajak, ngajak	*sareng*
woman	anak luh	*anak istri*
wood	kayu	*taru*
wooden tower in temple for a deity	mêru	
word	kruna	*suara*
work	ngaê (gaê)	*makarya (karya)*
worked out	gaêna	*karyananga*
world, earth	gumi	*jagat*
yard, courtyard	tengatah	
year	tiban	*warsa*
yellow	kuning	*jenar*
yellow rice	nasi bira	
yes, sure, really, right	aa	*patut*, *inggih*
yesterday	dibi	*ring dibi*
you	raganê	*jero*
young	nguda	*anom*

$1 = 33 \quad$ TAIWAN

$10 = 3.30$

$20 = 660$

$100. = 3,330$